100 GREATS

WEST BROMWICH ALBION FC

The author (right) with two former Albion captains, Ray Barlow (centre) and Graham Williams (left). Williams, a Welsh international player, and Barlow, who appeared for England, played in a total of 842 competitive games for Albion between them.

100 GREATS

WEST BROMWICH ALBION FC

TONY MATTHEWS

TEMPUS

First published 2001
Copyright © Tony Matthews, 2001

Tempus Publishing Limited
The Mill, Brimscombe Port,
Stroud, Gloucestershire, GL5 2QG

ISBN 0 7524 2224 3

Typesetting and origination by
Tempus Publishing Limited
Printed in Great Britain by
Midway Colour Print, Wiltshire

Also available from Tempus Publishing:

0 7524 2248 0	Accrington Stanley: Images	Phil Whalley	£10.99
0 7524 1862 9	Birmingham City: Images	Tony Matthews	£9.99
0 7524 2249 9	Bristol City 1967-2001: Images	Tom Hopegood	£10.99
0 7524 2068 2	Cardiff City 1971-2000: Images	Richard Shepherd	£9.99
0 7524 1545 X	Crewe Alexandra : Images	Harold Finch	£9.99
0 7524 2176 X	Crystal Palace: Greats	Revd Nigel Sands	£12.00
0 7524 2189 1	Doncaster Rovers: Images	Peter Tuffrey	£10.99
0 7524 2259 6	Everton 1880-1945: Images	John Rowlands	£10.99
0 7524 1855 6	The Football Programme	John Litster	£12.99
0 7524 2042 9	Forever England	Mark Shaoul & Tony Williamson	£16.99
0 7524 2243 X	Gillingham: Men Who Made	Roger Triggs	£19.99
0 7524 2152 2	Ipswich Town: Images	Tony Garnett	£9.99
0 7524 2043 7	Leeds United in Europe	David Saffer	£9.99
0 7524 2094 1	Leyton Orient: Images	Neilson Kaufman	£9.99
0 7524 2255 3	Manchester City: Classics	Andrew Waldon	£12.00
0 7524 2085 2	Manchester City: Images	David Saffer & Andrew Waldon	£9.99
0 7524 1849 1	Millwall 1884-1939: Images	Millwall FC Museum	£9.99
0 7524 2187 5	Millwall 1940-2001: Images	Millwall FC Museum	£10.99
0 7524 1671 5	Northampton Town: Images	John Watson & David Walden	£9.99
0 7524 2266 9	Norwich FC: Images	Gary Enderby	£10.99
0 7524 1604 9	Queens Park Rangers: Images	Tony Williamson	£9.99
0 7524 2081 X	Reading: Greats	David Downs	£12.00
0 7524 1670 7	Rotherham United: Images	Gerry Somerton	£9.99
0 7524 2264 2	Sheffield United: Greats	Denis Clarebrough	£12.00
0 7524 2177 8	Southend United: Greats	Peter Miles & Dave Goody	£12.00
0 7524 1133 0	Swansea Town 1912-1964: Images	Richard Shepherd	£9.99
0 7524 2093 3	Swindon Town: Images	Richard Mattick	£9.99
0 7524 2044 5	Tottenham Hotspur 1882-1952: Images	Roy Brazier	£9.99
0 7524 2091 7	Walsall: Images	Geoff Allman	£9.99
0 7524 2226 X	Walsall: Greats	Geoff Allman	£12.00
0 7524 2056 9	West Brom Albion: Images	Tony Matthews	£9.99
0 7524 2045 3	1966 World Cup	Norman Shiel	£9.99

INTRODUCTION

One of the oldest, and indeed truest, cliches in football is that the game is all about opinions. It follows, therefore, that the choice made by me regarding the hundred greatest players ever to have donned a West Bromwich Albion shirt is unlikely to coincide exactly with the choice of any other person ... although my great pal and fellow Albion fan Colin Mackenzie came mighty close with his own personal selection. Nevertheless, there will still be considerable debate as to the players I have included in, and those I have left out of, my 100 Albion greats – I could have certainly added another fifty stars without any trouble, but I was limited to only 100.

All the players who have made over 300 appearances for the club at senior level are included, and several more who achieved splendid goalscoring records are also featured. There are, of course, certain players I know would get into everyone's top fifty, including those listed on the front cover of this book. There are also the odd few players who spent only a short time at the club, yet did exceedingly well when they pulled on a navy blue and white striped shirt.

In the good old days, before League football was introduced, Albion had some tremendous players. Some have been included in this selection, others just missed out. But if they had been around twenty years later, then I am sure they would have figured as well. For instance, I have not included in my final choice the likes of George and Harry Bell, Tommy Green, Jack Horton, George Timmins and Joe Wilson from the 1880s, but I have named Billy Bassett, Jem Bayliss, Ezra Horton, Roddy McLeod, Tom Pearson, Charlie and Tom Perry, Joe Reader, Bob Roberts and George 'Spry' Woodhall.

Amos Adams, Jack Banks, Amos Dunn, Ben Garfield, Alf Geddes, Willie Groves, Harry Hadley, Tom Higgins, Abe Jones, Albert Flewitt, Sammy Nicholls, Jack 'Baldy' Reynolds and Billy Richards, who all gave Albion supreme service in the 1890s, can't get in either, but some of their colleagues can, among them Chippy Simmons and Billy Williams.

Then there are the stars from 1900 to 1915, namely George Baddeley, Fred Buck, Howard Gregory, Claude Jephcott, Bobby McNeal, Jack Manners, Fred Morris, Bob Pailor, goalkeeper Bert Pearson, Jesse 'Peerless' Pennington, Ted Pheasant, Arthur Randle, Fred Reed, Sammy Richardson, Fred Shinton and Joe Smith. But there is no room for Jimmy Stringer or Frank Waterhouse.

George Ashmore, Bobby Blood, Jack Byers, Ivor Jones, Arthur Perry and Fred Reed failed to make the list from the 1920s, but some exciting and talented goalscorers did: Joe Carter, Jimmy Cookson, Stan Davies, Tommy Glidden, George James and 'Tug' Wilson. Three of them also starred in the 1930s and became household names, playing alongside Jimmy 'Iron' Edwards, Bob Finch, Tommy Magee, Harold Pearson, Bill Richardson, 'W.G.' Richardson, Teddy Sandford, George Shaw, Bert Trentham and Stan Wood, all of whom were part of Albion's great double-winning side in 1930/31. Wally Boyes, Jimmy Murphy, Jack Rix, Walter Robbins, Jack Sankey and Cecil Shaw all played before the Second World War, likewise Ike Clarke and Sandy McNab, Joe Johnson and Harry 'Popeye' Jones. Most of these splendid players are featured in this book.

During the 1940s and '50s more quality players came to the fore, among them Ronnie Allen, Ray Barlow, Jimmy Dudley, Jimmy Dugdale, Billy Elliott, Frank Griffin, Norman Heath, Don Howe, Alec Jackson, Joe Kennedy, Derek Kevan, George Lee, Len Millard, Johnny Nicholls,

Jim Pemberton, Stan Rickaby, Bobby Robson, Paddy Ryan, Jim Sanders, Maurice Setters, Jack Vernon, Dave Walsh and Welsh internationals Graham and Stuart Williams. They all gave Albion excellent service.

It was the same throughout the 1960s, with Jeff Astle, Tony Brown, Clive Clark, Doug Fraser, Asa Hartford, Bobby Hope, Stan Jones, John Kaye, Graham Lovett, John Osborne, Ray Potter, John Talbut and Ray Wilson producing the goods. The stars of the 1970s included: Brendon Batson, Martyn Bennett, Ally Brown, Len Cantello, Laurie Cunningham, Johnny Giles, Tony Godden, Willie Johnston, Mick Martin, Paddy Mulligan, Cyrille Regis, Bryan Robson, Ally Robertson, Derek Statham and John Wile. These were followed by Peter Barnes, Don Goodman, Steve Mackenzie, Stuart Naylor, Gary Owen and Clive Whitehead.

More recently it was Daryl Burgess, Andy Hunt, Bernard McNally, Paul Raven, Gary Robson, Richard Sneekes, Gary Strodder and Bob Taylor, while today the fans are cheering for Neil Clement, Lee Hughes, Ruel Fox and Jason Roberts, among others.

I started compiling this book in 1997 and, over the last four years or so, I have added, omitted, amended facts and figures appertaining to so many players – players I have finally selected as my top 100 Albion greats. So many excellent players have been associated with West Bromwich Albion Football Club over the years – let's hope they can go on to get many more!

ACKNOWLEDGEMENTS

Firstly, I would like to thank Colin Mackenzie yet again for assisting me with this publication. He has been such a terrific aide over the past twenty-five years, contributing immensely to each and every book I have written and compiled on West Bromwich Albion FC. I have also taken snippets of information from various other sources, referring to articles, stories, books, magazines and newspapers appertaining to the Albion. Consequently, Glenn Willmore (editor) and John Homer (assistant editor) deserve a worthy of a mention for what they have written on various players via *The Baggies* newspaper.

I would like to thank my old buddy Laurie Rampling for the loan of some tremendous photographs, likewise local picture-taker Kevin Grice and London-based Barry Marsh, among others. Certain photographs have come directly from the Albion museum, some belong to the families of ex-players, some from players still with us today and several from other sources, including supporters, young and old. I thank you all.

Thanks too, to James Howarth of Tempus Publishing, who asked me to compile this book some time ago, following on from my pictorial history in the *Images of Sport* series, entitled *West Bromwich Albion: 100 Years at The Hawthorns*.

And last but not least, thank you again to my wife, Margaret, for allowing me to spend so much time on the keyboard and with my nose in all those reference books.

Up the Baggies!

Tony Matthews
Summer 2001

100 WEST BROMWICH ALBION GREATS

Ronnie Allen
Jeff Astle
George Baddeley
Ray Barlow
Billy Bassett
Brendon Batson
Jem Bayliss
Sid Bowser
Wally Boyes
Ally Brown
Tony Brown
Fred Buck
Len Cantello
Joe Carter
Clive Clark
Ike Clarke
Jimmy Cookson
Laurie Cunningham
Stan Davies
Jimmy Dudley
Jimmy Dugdale
Jimmy Edwards
Billy Elliott
Bob Finch
Doug Fraser
Johnny Giles
Tommy Glidden
Tony Godden
Don Goodman
Howard Gregory
Frank Griffin
Asa Hartford
Norman Heath
Bobby Hope

Ezra Horton
Don Howe
Lee Hughes
Andy Hunt
George James
Claude Jephcott
Willie Johnston
Stan Jones
John Kaye
Joe Kennedy
Derek Kevan
George Lee
Roddy McLeod
Bobby McNeal
Tommy Magee
Jack Manners
Len Millard
Fred Morris
Paddy Mulligan
Jimmy Murphy
Stuart Naylor
Johnny Nicholls
Dan Nurse
John Osborne
Gary Owen
Bob Pailor
Harold Pearson
Hubert Pearson
Tom Pearson
Jesse Pennington
Charlie Perry
Tom Perry
Ted Pheasant
Joe Reader

Cyrille Regis
Bill Richardson
'W.G.' Richardson
Sammy Richardson
Stan Rickaby
Bob Roberts
Ally Robertson
Bobby Robson
Bryan Robson
Reg Ryan
Jim Sanders
Teddy Sandford
Maurice Setters
George Shaw
Fred Shinton
Chippy Simmons
Joe Smith
Richard Sneekes
Derek Statham
John Talbut
Bob Taylor
Bert Trentham
Jack Vernon
Dave Walsh
Ike Webb
John Wile
Billy Williams
Graham Williams
Stuart Williams
Charlie Wilson
Stan Wood
George Woodhall

The top twenty, who appear here in italics, are all afforded extra coverage.

Ronnie Allen

Outside-right/centre forward, 1950-61

Football League:	415	208
FA Cup:	42	23
Other:	1	3
Total:	458	234

Born in Fenton, Stoke-on-Trent in January 1929, Ronnie Allen was successfully converted from a speedy outside-right into a goalscoring centre forward of the highest calibre. West Bromwich Albion manager Jack Smith was the man mainly responsible for switching Allen from the wing, doing so during the 1951/52 season on the recommendation of ex-team captain and director Tommy Glidden and Irish international centre-half Jack Vernon.

Allen possessed a powerful shot in both feet; he was a superb volleyer of the ball and a top-class penalty-taker (he netted over 40 times from the spot during his career). In the words of the late Sir Stanley Matthews, he was 'The Complete Footballer'. Despite his height (5ft 8in) Allen was also a very good header of the ball and often rose above his opponent to be first to a well-driven or well-flighted centre.

After doing very well on the right-wing for Port Vale (he scored 40 goals in more than 150 first team appearances for the Potteries club during and immediately after the Second World War), Allen became Albion's record signing in March 1950, costing the club £20,000. It was money well spent. He made a goalscoring debut for the Baggies against Black Country rivals Wolves in front of a record Hawthorns' League attendance of 60,945, just twenty-four hours after joining the club. But Allen could easily have missed that local derby. An efficient steward, not recognising Albion's new recruit, refused to let him into the ground – until the club secretary was called to vouch for him!

Allen scored regularly in each of his eleven seasons with the Baggies, finishing with a record tally of 234 goals in all competitive matches (with 208 of these coming in League competition, beating the previous best of 202 achieved by 'W.G.' Richardson). Allen's record was to remain for seventeen years until Tony Brown bettered it in 1978.

Allen took over the number nine shirt from Irish international Dave Walsh, and in 1953/54 he and his strike partner, Johnny Nicholls (together they were known as the 'Terrible Twins'), between them scored 66 goals, helping Albion win the FA Cup and finish runners-up to Wolves in the First Division title race.

When Vic Buckingham, the former Spurs full-back, took over the reins at The Hawthorns he got Allen to pull the marking centre-half out of the defence by quickly switching from the centre to the wing, thus allowing Nicholls to dart through the middle. It was a plan that worked to

Ronnie Allen thwarted by Arsenal's Welsh international goalkeeper Jack Kelsey during a League game at Highbury in 1953.

perfection for three seasons before Nicholls moved on. Derek Kevan and Bobby Robson then came in to join Allen in Albion's forward line and the trio, with Allen instrumental in creating chances, rattled in over 170 goals.

On leaving The Hawthorns, Allen became player-coach at Selhurst Park and then took up a coaching appointment with Baggies' arch enemy, Wolves. He began his managerial career at Molineux (January 1966-December 1968) and moved to Athletic Bilbao (March 1969-November 1971), Sporting Lisbon (April 1972-May 1973) and Walsall (June-December 1973). He returned to The Hawthorns as Albion's manager (June-December 1977, after a spell as their scouting advisor), but left to coach Saudi Arabia's national team. He managed Panathiniakos from June to September 1980 and then returned to Albion, which he managed from July 1981 until May 1982. He spent the next season as Albion's

general manager.

He guided Wolves back into the First Division in 1967, and led Bilbao to victory in the Spanish Cup final and also to the runners-up spot in the League (behind Atletico Madrid). He also took Albion to two semi-finals in 1982 (they lost both, to Spurs in the League Cup and to QPR in the FA Cup).

Following a spell out of the game, when he worked as a sales director for a Black Country engineering firm and attempted to get onto the Albion board of directors, Allen returned to The Hawthorns as a coach. He retained his position until illness ended his soccer activities in 1997, just two years after he had played his last game of football – a friendly match for Albion against Cheltenham Town – at the age of 66 years, 115 days. Sadly, Allen died in June 2001, aged seventy-two.

Allen's son, Russell, was an Albion reserve during the early 1970s before moving to Tranmere Rovers and later Mansfield Town.

Football League:	290+2	137
FA Cup:	23	14
League Cup:	28	19
Europe:	10	1
Other:	8	3
Total:	359+2	174

Jeff Astle holds a record that will never be beaten! In May 1968 he fired home an extra-time winner for West Bromwich Albion in the FA Cup final versus Everton. Two years later, in March 1970, he headed the Baggies into an early lead over Manchester City in the League Cup final, and therefore had the distinction of becoming the first player to score in each of those major two finals at Wembley.

Scoring goals was Astle's business, and during an excellent career he netted 213 in 480 competitive matches for his two Football League clubs: Notts County and the Albion. Astle once remarked (during an interview in 1993) that 'I enjoyed every minute of my playing career. I wouldn't have changed it for the world and if I had the opportunity to do it all over again, I would do so without hesitation.'

Born in Eastwood, Nottingham in May 1942, he played for Trinity Youth Club, West Notts Boys and John Player FC before joining Notts County as an amateur, turning professional at Meadow Lane in July 1960. After four excellent years with the Magpies, partly under the watchful eye of former England centre forward Tommy Lawton, Astle was transferred to The Hawthorns in September 1964 for what was to prove a bargain fee of just £25,000 – an astute piece of business by manager Jimmy Hagan.

The fans took to him immediately, especially after he had scored twice in an emphatic 5-1 win over arch-rivals Wolves on his home debut. He formed a fine partnership up front with John Kaye and had Tony 'Bomber' Brown aiding and abetting from midfield. He never really looked back after that. Nicknamed 'The King', Astle developed into a tremendous striker, superb in the air and not at all bad on the ground. He went on to register 174 goals in 361 first-class appearances for Albion, helping them win the League Cup in 1966, the FA Cup in 1968 and also reach two other League Cup finals (in 1967 and 1970). He twice scored two hat-tricks in the space of a few days – in September 1965 v. Northampton Town and Sheffield Wednesday and in April 1968 v. West Ham United and Manchester United. The latter two clubs had several mean defenders in their ranks at the time, with the Old Trafford Reds just winding themselves up

Jeff Astle heading home one of his three goals in Albion's 4-2 home League win over Sheffield Wednesday in September 1965.

to take hold of the European Cup.

He gained 5 England caps (1969 and 1970), had outings for the Football League XI and the England 'B' team. In 1968 he was voted Midlands Footballer of the Year. As a member of England's World Cup squad in Mexico in 1970, he had the misfortune, after coming on as a substitute, to miss a sitter with the scoresheet blank. Astle later recalled 'I should have scored, there was no excuse.' Goalkeeper Gordon Banks, talking after the game, said that God had been on his side when he saved Pele's header, but He wasn't on Jeff's.

After a deserved testimonial match in 1974,

Astle left Albion to join the South African club, Hellenic. On his return to England he wound down his career with spells at Dunstable, Weymouth, Atherstone Town and Hillingdon Borough before retiring in 1978 after a few outings for the Albion Old Stars XI. A self-employed industrial cleaner, he also appeared regularly on the *Fantasy Football League* show with the comedians Frank Skinner and David Baddiel and then ran his own 'Road Show'. Unfortunately, Astle hasn't been too well of late but his playing career with Albion will remain in the memories of the supporters for the rest of their lives.

George Baddeley
Right-half, 1908-14

Football League:	145	1
FA Cup:	12	0
Total:	157	1

Right-half George 'Stodger' Baddeley is the oldest player ever to have lined up in a Football League match for West Bromwich Albion. He was aged 39 years and 345 days when he made his final appearance for the club, against Sheffield Wednesday at The Hawthorns on 18 April 1914. Strong in all aspects of defensive play, he had earlier skippered Stoke, for whom he starred in 225 first-class fixtures between 1901 and 1908.

Born at Feggs Hayes, North Staffordshire (near Stoke-on-Trent) in May 1874, he learnt his football with Pitshill & Biddulph FC before embarking on a professional career at The Victoria Ground. On his arrival at Albion he went straight into the first team, playing in front of Jesse Pennington and alongside tough-nut centre-half Ted Pheasant. Baddeley was a credit to the side. His tackles were hard but fair, he was always involved in the action and was a key member of Albion's Second Division Championship-winning side of 1910/11. The following season he was again instrumental on the field of play as the Baggies reached the FA Cup final, only to lose after a replay to Barnsley.

Baddeley was outstanding in both games against Barnsley and in the replay he almost won Albion the Cup – sadly, his tremendous twenty-five yard drive flew inches over the bar. Five minutes later, the referee blew the whistle. The game went into extra time and although Albion had the better of the exchanges, the Tykes snatched victory with what was virtually the last kick of the game, Harry Tufnell racing clear of Jesse Pennington to fire past Hubert Pearson.

In 1912/13, Baddeley made only ten League appearances (due to the emergence of Frank Waterhouse) and was largely used as a reserve for the next two seasons, before deciding to retire at the end of the 1913/14 season. He remained at The Hawthorns as first-team coach until competitive football was suspended due to the First World War.

Baddeley was strong and purposeful in possession, tough and resilient in the tackle and forever urging his colleagues on. He never waned, and always gave 100 per cent (no matter what the circumstances). He made almost 160 senior appearances for Albion and scored just one goal, a real beauty struck from distance in a 2-0 win at Glossop North End in December 1910.

When peacetime football returned in 1919, Baddeley was a regular supporter at The Hawthorns and he was as delighted as anyone when the First Division Championship was won in 1920. He later became a publican in West Bromwich, the town where he died in July 1952 at the age of seventy-eight.

Ray Barlow

Inside forward/wing-half, 1944-60

Football League:	403	31
FA Cup:	46	5
Other:	33	12
Total:	482	48

A tall, long-striding, rangy player, Ray Barlow was spotted by the former West Bromwich Albion goalscorer Jimmy Cookson playing for the Wiltshire intermediate works side Garrards FC, who employed him as an engineer. He was quickly recommended to The Hawthorns, signing amateur forms in June 1944 and turning professional five months later.

Able to occupy a variety of positions, including all three in the half-back line and the three central forward roles, Barlow was undoubtedly at his best in the left-half berth and was, in some people's minds, the finest player Albion have ever had in that position. He was described in some quarters as a second Charlie Buchan.

After scoring 10 goals in 32 games during the 1945/46 transitional season – when clubs were slowly getting back to normality after the Second World War – Barlow made only 10 League appearances in 1946/47 before completing his National Service, serving as a gunner in the Tank Regiment in the Middle East.

He returned to England in April 1948 and scored in the last Central League game of the season against Chesterfield. But, after starting the next campaign in the senior side, he then had to bide his time in the reserves while Cyril Williams, Jack Haines, Len Millard and Glyn Hood occupied the two inside forward and wing-half positions respectively. With promotion there for the taking, injuries and lack of form (on the part of a couple of players) resulted in manager Jack Smith making changes to his side. Barlow was brought back in mid-January and he held firm, becoming a key member of the side, playing at right-half and as an inside forward as Albion took second spot in the division (behind Fulham). Thereafter, Barlow was an integral part of Vic Buckingham's team of the mid-1950s, when Albion were regarded as one of the best footballing sides in the country.

Playing some twenty yards behind the attack-minded forward line, he was able to bring the ball down from unusual heights with his long legs and nonchalantly spray sweeping, diagonal passes across the field with great precision, bringing his wingers into the game with one swift movement. Indeed, he could pick out a player some forty or fifty yards away with pinpoint accuracy.

Barlow, who was born in Swindon in August 1926, was extremely unlucky not to have won more England caps than the one he did receive, against Northern Ireland in 1954. This was mainly due to the exceptional form of Portsmouth's Jimmy Dickinson. But nevertheless, he was next best in the left-half position for at least four seasons, often being named as reserve to the national team.

He eventually took over the centre half position at The Hawthorns from Joe Kennedy and from here he captained the side, leading

them into the FA Cup semi-finals in 1957. Three years earlier, in the Cup Final against Preston North End, he had been brought down inside the penalty area by Tommy Docherty after one of his surging runs; Ronnie Allen stepped up to level the scores at 2-2 and, with Barlow dominant, Albion went on to lift the trophy.

During the period 1953 to 1958, Barlow was quite outstanding. Only injury and international duties kept him out of the first team and when Albion toured, and indeed won, in Russia in the summer of 1957, he was acclaimed as 'the finest English footballer' to play behind the Iron Curtain. His powerful runs often bemused the usually reliable Soviet defenders and after the opening game versus FC Zenit (which ended in a 1-1 draw) Barlow was widely applauded by the 80,000 crowd, who even threw him flowers!

Three years earlier he had performed wonderfully well in midfield alongside some of the famous Hungarians when Albion lost 5-3 to Honved in the Le Soir International Festival in Brussels. Barlow matched and even bettered the likes of Puskas, Bozsik, Lorant and Kocsis for well over an hour until he badly injured his leg (the same limb he had damaged playing for England the week before).

After more than 400 competitive games for Albion, Barlow left The Hawthorns in the summer of 1960 and joined neighbours Birmingham City and, after a season with Stourbridge (1961/62), finally hung up his boots with well over 500 major appearances under his belt.

Barlow, who ran a confectionery and tobacconists shop in West Bromwich (formerly owned by 1930s skipper Tommy Glidden) later took charge of a post office in Stourbridge. He played in several charity matches for the Albion Old Stars until finally calling it a day in 1990. He now resides in Pedmore, near Stourbridge.

Billy Basset

Outside right, 1886-99

Football League:	261	61
FA Cup:	40	11
Other:	10	5
Total:	311	77

Billy Bassett, one of the great names in the history of West Bromwich Albion Football Club and, indeed, in English footballing circles, was a flying right-winger who, besides electrifying pace, had tremendous on-the-ball skills, packed a fierce shot in his right-foot and always enjoyed the big occasion. He tried to hug the touchline as much as possible, taking on and beating his full-back on the outside with sheer pace before delivering a telling cross, hit high or low into the danger zone.

Besides creating openings for his colleagues, he was also a superb marksman himself and when the ball was on the opposite flank he would always venture in towards the centre of the field, where he regularly snapped up the half-chances that came his way.

Born in West Bromwich in January 1869, Bassett joined Albion in August 1886 from West Bromwich (Trinity) Strollers, whom he had captained the previous season when he also played a game or two for Oak Villa and for Albion's third team (March 1886).

His career lasted thirteen years and during that time he was capped 16 times by England, and manfully starred in eight internationals against Scotland. He also represented the Football League side and the FA XI, and lined up in three FA Cup finals for Albion – 1888, 1892 and 1895. He gained a winners' medal in the first encounter at The Kennington Oval against Preston North End, when his impressive display led to him receiving his initial cap at the age of nineteen.

Bassett formed a fine right-wing partnership with fellow England international George Woodhall and, with Ezra Horton often behind him, Albion's right flank was one of the most impressive in the country during the late 1880s. Even after Horton and Woodhall had departed, Bassett continued to impress down the wing with Scotsman Roddy McLeod his inside right and John 'Baldy' Reynolds and then Tom Perry occupying the wing-half position.

Bassett went on to appear in more than 300 first-class games for Albion (scoring over 75 goals) before electing to hang up his boots at the end of the 1898/99 season, following a crushing 7-1 defeat at Villa Park – his last game for the club.

At that point Bassett went into business locally before returning to The Hawthorns as a director in March 1905, moving up to become chairman in September 1908. He served in that capacity until his death in West Bromwich in April 1937 – just two days before Albion were due to play Preston

North End in the FA Cup semi-final at Highbury. Albion lost that semi-final showdown 4-1 and, after the game, centre half Teddy Sandford said: 'We were all too full up to play. Mr Bassett's death stunned the whole team — even the supporters. He was such a well-respected person. He taught me a lot and I must admit that I was tearful for most of the first half following the minute's silence before the kick-off.'

Over 100,000 mourners paid tribute to one of Albion's greatest servants and *Pathe News* even covered the funeral procession, which started at The Hawthorns and went straight into West Bromwich town centre before making its way to the cemetery.

Bassett, who was associated with the Albion for fifty-one years, was a member of the Football League Management Committee and an FA Council member (1930-37); he was also on the FA's International Selection Committee (1936-37) and was a Justice of the Peace (appointed in 1935).

Brendon Batson

Right-back, 1978-84

Football League:	172	1
FA Cup:	13	1
League Cup:	21	0
Europe:	12	0
Other:	2	0
Total:	220	2

Brendon Batson was a very efficient right-back, always eager to get forward and give assistance to his wide midfielders and inside forwards. Born in the Windward Islands, at St George in Grenada in February 1953, and educated in London, where he gained three GCEs, he subsequently joined Arsenal on schoolboy forms before turning professional at Highbury in June 1971.

After recieving an FA Youth Cup winners' medal, he failed to establish himself in the Gunners' League side and, as a result, moved to Cambridge United in January 1974. Here he came into contact with manager Ron Atkinson, who made him United captain and led them to the Fourth Division Championship in 1977. Atkinson then took charge of West Bromwich Albion and he made Batson his first Hawthorns signing in February 1978 for £30,000.

Batson's best season was 1978/79. He missed only one League game and formed a magnificent full-back partnership with Derek Statham. Indeed, he and Statham were certainly good enough to have played together for England.

Bitterly disappointed when Albion lost to Red Star Belgrade in the quarter-finals of the UEFA Cup in 1979, Batson had the misfortune to be 'as sick as a pig' again when Albion were beaten in two major cup semi-finals in a matter of seven weeks in 1982, going down 1-0 (on aggregate) to Tottenham Hotspur in the League Cup and 1-0 to Queen's Park Rangers in the FA Cup.

Steady, easy-going and sincere, Batson went on to play in well over 200 games for the Baggies, appearing in the UEFA Cup and gaining 3 England 'B' caps in 1980. Sadly in 1984, on doctor's advice, he retired from competitive football with a serious knee injury.

Albion immediately granted him a testimonial match to say 'thank you' for six years' splendid service. He assisted the Albion Old Stars and Witton Albion for a while before joining the PFA, where he has remained ever since, initially as assistant-secretary, then as a senior member of the staff under chief executive Gordon Taylor. Now he is deputy chief executive of the PFA.

Batson was awarded the MBE in the New Year's Honours List in January 2001.

Football League:	56	12
FA Cup:	39	24
Total:	95	36

James Bayliss was known throughout his career as 'Jem' – the initials of three of his four Christian names, the others being Edward and Matthias. He was a grand all-round footballer, always full of running, a willing, tireless worker and a player who often came up with a spectacular goal (or two) with either foot or his head. He possessed a powerful shot and often tried his luck with some direct, long range shooting. Bayliss occupied the right-half, inside right and centre forward positions for West Bromwich Albion, preferring to lead the attack, which he did with both style and skill.

Born in Tipton in August 1863, he played his early football at Great Bridge and Horseley Heath schools, and then assisted Great Bridge Unity, Tipton Providence and Wednesbury Old Athletic before joining Albion in August 1884, turning professional twelve months later after guesting for Walsall Town. He scored twice on his senior debut against Derby Junction (away) in an FA Cup-tie in October 1884 – the first of 36 goals he was to claim for the Throstles in 95 competitive games up to his retirement in May 1892. He actually joined the board of directors in 1891 while still an active player and served in that capacity until 1905, when he was replaced in office by his former playing colleague, Billy Bassett.

Bayliss scored around 25 goals in his first season with the club (all games), and did likewise the following season – when he claimed his first hat-trick versus Old Westminsters in the FA Cup – and weighed in with 40 goals in 1886/87 before topping the 50 mark the following campaign.

Bayliss was a rare gem when it came to hitting the target and finding a way past the opposition goalkeeper, and all told it is believed he scored around 150 goals for Albion before League Football came into being in 1888. He linked up superbly well with Bassett and George 'Spry' Woodhall and also with Tom Pearson during the late 1880s.

Bayliss played in three successive FA Cup finals – 1886 (v. Blackburn Rovers), 1887 (v. Aston Villa) and 1888 (v. Preston North End). He was on the losing side in the first two, but then grabbed the first goal in the Preston final as Albion pulled off a terrific 2-1 victory over the red-hot favourites from Deepdale. Capped once by England (v. Ireland in 1891) Bayliss – a gentleman in more ways than one – read his own obituary notice in a local newspaper in 1897 after returning from a holiday in Gibralter. While he was abroad rumours circulated around his home area of Great Bridge that he had died of typhoid fever. Nothing could have been further from the truth … he returned fit and well and lived for a further thirty-six years. He subsequently had the notice framed and hung it in his living room for posterity.

Bayliss, one of Albion's finest club men, died in West Bromwich on 19 August 1933, three days after his seventieth birthday.

Sid Bowser

Inside left/centre half, 1903-13 and 1914-24

Football League:	341	64
FA Cup:	28	8
Other:	2	-
Total:	371	72

Sid Bowser was a tenacious and resilient footballer, who was able to occupy either the centre half or inside left positions. As a defender he was hard-working, strong in the tackle, competitive and, above all, as solid as a rock. When playing in the front-line he was alert, aggressive and able to adapt to the circumstances without any problems whatsoever. Indeed, he was certainly a tremendous attacker and goalscorer during the first of his two separate spells at The Hawthorns.

Born in January 1892 in Handsworth, within walking distance of the ground, Bowser played his early football with Astbury Richmond and Willenhall and had an unsuccessful trial with Birmingham before joining Albion in July 1908, turning professional six months later.

He scored twice on his senior debut for the club against Grimsby Town (at home) in a Second Division game in January 1909 (to celebrate his seventeenth birthday) and never looked back after that, despite leaving the club for ten months (between April 1913 and February 1914) when he went over to Ireland to play for Belfast Distillery.

Prior to his departure, Bowser had helped Albion win the Second Division Championship in 1910/11 when he was part of a very impressive forward line, usually constituted of: Billy Wollaston, himself, Bob Pailor, Fred Buck and Amos Lloyd. Bowser scored 22 League goals that

term, forming a fine striking partnership through the middle with Pailor. The following season Bowser was in the Albion side that reached the FA Cup final only to lose 1-0 in a replay to Barnsley.

Soon after his return to the club he took over the centre half berth from Fred Buck, who had moved there halfway through the 1911/12 campaign. And what a great move it was for both club and player, as Bowser became the fulcrum at the heart of the Baggies' defence, playing splendidly between Frank Waterhouse and Bobby McNeal and in front of two excellent full-backs, Joe Smith and England's Jesse Pennington.

During the First World War he guested for Notts County and Southport Vulcan and, after the hostilities had ended and now with Sammy Richardson as his right-half colleague, he was prominent as Albion won the First Division title in style in 1919/20, amassing a record 60 points and scoring over 100 goals. Bowser converted eight penalties that season, two going towards a hat-trick in a 4-1 home win over Bradford City (giving him the honour of being the first Albion defender ever to claim three goals in a competitive match).

After scoring over 70 goals in more than 370 senior appearances for the Baggies, he was transferred from the club for a second time in August 1924, moving to neighbouring Walsall, with whom he remained for three years before retiring in 1927 to become a publican in Dudley, remaining in the trade for twenty-five years.

Capped once by England against Ireland in 1919, Bowser also represented the Irish League whilst with Distillery. He died in Birmingham in 1961.

Wally Boyes

Football League:	151	35
FA Cup:	14	3
Total:	165	38

Wally Boyes was initially an inside forward who was converted into a fast-raiding left-winger before moving to left-half. Standing only 5ft 5in tall – which makes him one of the smallest players ever to don an Albion shirt – he had good, close ball control, could shoot with both feet and crossed an excellent ball on the run. He overcame the additional handicap of having one leg shorter than the other and scored some crucial goals as well as making plenty more for his colleagues.

Boyes was born in the Yorkshire village of Killamarsh, in January 1913, and as a schoolboy prodigy in Sheffield he once scored 17 goals in a game which his team (Netherthorpe Council School) won 31-2. Late on in that game he fell foul of the referee when claiming a late penalty – such was his enthusiasm for football.

Boyes was a clever player, although some felt that on occasions he was far too intricate and would have preferred him to be more direct. Nevertheless, he gave Albion excellent service over a period of seven years (from February 1931 to February 1938). He made his senior debut in front of 60,000 fans in the local derby against Aston Villa at The Hawthorns in November 1931 when he took over at inside-left from Teddy Sandford.

Boyes made 17 appearances in the League side that season (occupying four different positions) but was then a reserve throughout the 1932/33 campaign before rejoining the senior ranks on a regular basis in January 1934, when he took over from Stan Wood on the left wing. He missed only one game in 1934/35, when he helped Albion reach the FA Cup final. He scored at Wembley that day but to no avail as the Baggies succumbed 4-2 to his boyhood favourites Sheffield Wednesday.

After more than 160 outings for Albion, Boyes – who won 4 England caps in total – was transferred to Everton, where he became part of one of the most impudent flank combinations ever seen at Goodison Park when partnering Alex Stephenson on the left. In 1938/39 he was outstanding as the Merseysiders won the First Division Championship, Boyes himself scoring 8 goals in 41 appearances.

Having guested for several clubs during the war, including Brentford, Leeds United, Manchester United, Newcastle, Preston and Sunderland, Boyes remained with Everton until 1949. Thereafter he wound down his career with spells at Notts County (as player-coach) and Scunthorpe United (player-trainer). He then took over as manager of Retford Town, holding a similar position with Hyde United before ending his footballing days as trainer with Swansea Town in 1959. He died in 1960 after a short illness.

Alistair Brown

Striker, 1972-83

Football League:	254+25	72
FA Cup:	26+2	6
League Cup:	27	2
Europe:	10	1
Other:	14+1	4
Total:	331+28	85

A versatile forward, who always gave a good, honest account of himself no matter what the circumstances, Alistair Brown was a true professional who enjoyed scoring goals. He found the net in each of his first two outings for Albion following his unusual £61,111 transfer from Leicester City on March 1972 (signed by manager Don Howe). He went on to become Albion's leading marksmen in 1975/76 (when promotion was gained from the Second Division under Johnny Giles) with 11 goals and again in 1978/79 (when the Baggies came so close to reaching the UEFA Cup final) with a total of 28. Brown was named joint Midland Footballer of the Year with his namesake, Tony, in this season.

During his time at The Hawthorns, Brown had several strike partners up front, but he got on with them all and, besides claiming over 80 goals in more than 350 games for Albion, he made many opportunities for his colleagues. He had a couple of lean years under Howe but overall did exceedingly well for the club, never feeling unwanted, and always there when required.

A Scotsman, born in Musselburgh in April 1951, he had joined Leicester City as a professional in April 1968 after eighteen months as an apprentice. He notched up 35 goals in 121 first-team appearances for the Foxes and was their chief marksman when they won the Second Division Championship in 1971.

Brown had made a dream start to his League career at Filbert Street, scoring twice on his debut against Sunderland in May 1969 – just prior to attending Wembley to watch his side lose in the FA Cup final to Manchester City. He gained Scottish youth caps and was an Under-23 international trialist before establishing himself in the City first team.

After a loan spell in Canada with Portland Timbers in 1981, Brown left The Hawthorns to sign for Crystal Palace in March 1983. He then retreated to the middle-line before rounding off his career with spells at Walsall and Port Vale, helping the latter club win promotion from the Fourth Division in his final playing season, 1985/86. Brown finished his career with 141 goals in 495 League appearances. He is now steward of the Albion supporters club in Halfords Lane, near to the ground.

Football League:	561+13	218
FA Cup:	53+1	27
League Cup:	46+1	17
Europe:	16+1	8
Other:	28	9
Total:	704+16	279

Albion's record appearance-maker and champion goalscorer, Tony 'Bomber' Brown, gave the club over twenty years of excellent service from April 1961 to October 1981. He gave so many sparkling performances in that time that one would require many more pages to elaborate on them in suitable detail. He was a player's player, always eager to get on with the game, never relaxing, forever buzzing around, seeking out scoring opportunities and creating openings for his colleagues with his off-the-ball runs and inter-changing tactics. He was unflagging in his approach to a game.

Brown occupied the right-half and all forward line positions for the Baggies and even kept goal on a couple of occasions in an emergency, but the fans will always remember him as an attacking midfielder, coming from deep positions to feed off his main strikers – Jeff Astle, Joe Mayo, David Cross, Alistair Brown and Cyrille Regis were just some of the players he linked up so well with. Brown packed a devastating right-foot shot and he wasn't bad with his left either. He netted some stunning goals from all angles and he put away over 50 penalties for Albion, missing only a handful. He overtook Ronnie Allen's scoring record of 208 League goals for Albion in 1978 with a cracker at Leeds. He went on to claim almost 280 at competitive level and, if one was to add in his 'friendly and tour' goals, his overall tally for the club stands at 312 (in 819 games) – a record which one doubts will ever be beaten. He has also starred in more games at The Hawthorns (361) than any other player.

Brown made 459 appearances for Albion in the First Division alone, played in 145 Cup matches (both records) and actually netted at least one goal in each of his eighteen seasons with the club, following his scoring League debut against Ipswich Town at Portman Road in September 1963. He was the First Division's leading striker, with 28 goals, in 1970/71.

Brown, a League Cup and FA Cup winner with Albion in 1966 and 1968 respectively, also played in two League Cup final defeats (1967 and 1970) and gained just one England cap (*v.* Wales at Wembley in 1971). He also represented England Youth and the Football League, and was voted Midland Footballer of the Year on three separate occasions: 1969, 1971 and 1979. On this final occasion the honour was shared with his team-mate Ally Brown).

A Lancastrian, born in Oldham in October 1945, Brown joined Albion as a junior in 1961 and turned professional in October 1963, after

making his senior debut. He played briefly for the Jacksonville & New England Teamen in 1980 and 1981 before transferring to Torquay United from where he switched to Stafford Rangers, ending his career in 1983. Brown returned to The Hawthorns as coach, under Giles (1984-86), and he also took a similar position with neighbouring Birmingham City (1987-89).

Granted three testimonials during his career (two by Albion), 'The Bomber' is definitely one of Albion's all time greats.

Fred Buck

Inside forward/centre half, 1900-03 and 1906-14

Football League:	287	90
FA Cup:	32	4
Total:	319	94

Fred Buck was only 5ft 5in tall, but he never let his height or indeed his weight (10 st 10 lb) bother him as he battled it out with the toughest and roughest players in the game. A resilient footballer and totally committed, he was one of Albion's many 'little' men who served the club during the early part of the twentieth century. A big-hearted player, lively in his actions, he possessed a lot of skill and courage and, above all, never gave less than his absolute best out on the field. Born in Newcastle-under-Lyne (Staffordshire) in July 1888, he played as an inside forward for Stafford Rangers before joining Albion in November 1900 – and what a superb start he made to his career at The Hawthorns, scoring on his debut when Albion whipped Bolton 7-2 at home.

Unfortunately, Albion were relegated at the end of that season, but they bounced back as Second Division Champions at the first attempt, although Buck hardly figured in the side. He made only 13 League appearances the following season before being transferred to Liverpool in May 1903.

He moved from Merseyside to Plymouth Argyle in March 1904, but then returned to The Hawthorns for a second spell in April 1906. This time he established himself in the first team straightaway and, over the next five seasons, played exceedingly well, scoring plenty of goals and helping Albion win promotion in 1910/11. It was his vital penalty in the last fixture of that season (at home to Huddersfield Town) which gave Albion a 1-0 victory and with it the Second Division title. At the start of the 1911/12 season, Buck was occupying the inside left berth, but halfway through the campaign he switched to right-half, taking over in the centre half position within a month. Here he became an tremendous competitor, and played with resilience and professionalism up to May 1914 when he transferred to Swansea Town, finally retiring in 1917.

One of the smallest centre halves ever to appear in an FA Cup final, he played his heart out in both games against Barnsley in April 1912. The first encounter finished level at 0-0 and it was stalemate again until the very last minute of extra time in the replay. Buck then stood and watched, unable to make a challenge, as Tufnell, the Barnsley forward, raced clear, past skipper Pennington, to score the winning goal and break Albion's hearts.

Buck, who twice represented the Football League in 1911/12, was a publican for twenty-four years after the First World War. He died in Stafford in June 1952.

Len Cantello
Midfield, 1967-79

Football League:	297+4	13
FA Cup:	22	3
League Cup:	21	3
Europe:	7	-
Other:	18	2
Total:	365+4	21

Len Cantello carried out many duties for West Bromwich Albion, donning ten different shirts for the First XI alone. He occupied the full-back, wing-half and inside forward positions mainly and, indeed, it was as a steadfast, stylish and hard-working midfielder where he performed best of all. A very competent footballer, he was born in Newton Heath, Manchester in September 1950 and joined Albion straight from school, turning professional in October 1968. Capped 6 times by England schoolboys, he then won 4 youth caps and later appeared in 8 under-23 internationals for his country. He teamed up in Albion's centre initially with Asa Hartford and Bobby Hope and played in the 1970 League Cup final before being aided and abetted in the engine-room by Bryan Robson, Remi Moses, Mick Martin, John Trewick and Johnny Giles.

For a midfielder, his strike record was not brilliant (as even he would admit) but he did score some stunning goals, none better that his net-bursting effort at Old Trafford in December 1978, when an eight-goal thriller between Manchester United and Albion finished 5-3 to the Baggies. Cantello's first-half right-foot rocket at the Stretford End (set up by Cyrille Regis's deft back-heeler) was later voted Goal of the Season.

He also scored a crackerjack in a 7-1 demolition of Coventry City at The Hawthorns in October 1978 and claimed another beauty in a 2-0 win over Middlesbrough later that same year.

Possessing a strong tackle and powerful right-foot shot, Cantello helped Albion gain promotion from the Second Division in 1976 and starred in European competition before moving to Bolton Wanderers in a £350,000 transfer deal soon after his testimonial in May 1979. Thereafter he assisted Eastern Athletic (Hong Kong), Burnley, Altrincham, Stafford Rangers, Hereford United, Bury, FC Cambuur (Holland), Peterborough United and Northwich Victoria before becoming assistant manager (to his former Albion colleague Asa Hartford) at Stockport County in 1987. He later scouted for Peterborough and Wigan Athletic and also managed Radcliffe Borough.

Football League:	414	145
FA Cup:	37	10
Total:	451	155

Joe Carter gave West Bromwich Albion fifteen years of excellent service from the inside right position. Upright and physically strong, with a long stride, he was good on the ball, possessed a powerful right-foot shot and, above all, was a real workhorse, covering acres of ground in every game he played. Born in enemy territory (Aston, Birmingham) in April 1901, he joined Albion as a professional in 1921 and made his League debut against Bolton Wanderers the following year – the first of more than 450 appearances for the club.

Carter formed a splendid partnership with Tommy Glidden on the right wing and 'The Twins', as they were called, lined up in more than 350 senior matches together, scoring plenty of goals as well as making many more for their colleagues.

Carter averaged one goal in every three games for Albion and was a key member of the club's successful, double-winning side in 1930/31 when victory in the FA Cup final and promotion from the Second Division were achieved in the same season. He also lined up in the 1935 Cup Final, although he was not fully match fit, and this time ended on the losing side.

Carter's best scoring campaign was in the Second Division season of 1929/30, when he netted 19 out of Albion's 105 goals, although he played in only 27 of the 42 League matches.

Prior to that he grabbed all of Albion's goals in an emphatic 4-0 League win at home over Tottenham Hotspur in December 1923. He hit a brilliant hat-trick in a 4-0 win over Manchester City in April 1933, following on in February 1935 with what was perhaps his best ever FA Cup goal, a bullet of a shot – albeit wind-assisted – in a 5-0 victory at Stockport.

He could – and would – have played in any forward position for Albion, but inside right was undoubtedly his best. Capped 3 times by England (1926-29), he also played for the Football League XI and starred in 3 international trials. He originally left Albion for Sheffield Wednesday in February 1936, but the deal fell through on medical grounds, leaving Carter free to join Tranmere Rovers for £450.

From there he switched to Walsall before retiring in 1942 after a short spell as player-manager of Vono Sports. He later became a publican in Handsworth, the town where he died in January 1977.

Clive Clark

Outside left, 1961-69

Football League:	300+1	80
FA Cup:	25+1	7
League Cup:	19	10
Europe:	7	1
Total:	31+2	98

Clive 'Chippy' Clark was a fast, direct goalscoring left-winger with skill and an appetite for the game. A Yorkshireman, born in Leeds in December 1940, he had trials with Huddersfield Town before going to Elland Road in 1957, transferring to Queens Park Rangers a year later and then on to West Bromwich Albion in January 1961 for what was to prove a bargain fee of just £17,000.

Clark made an impressive debut as Albion beat Preston North End 3-1 at The Hawthorns. The crowd took to him at once and although he only claimed one goal that season, it proved to be a decisive one, the winner against Leicester City.

He had the knack of being able to get into the penalty area when least expected. The ball would be out on the right, even locked in defence, but all it took was two sweeping passes, one centre and Clark was there, in with a chance of scoring a goal.

He was brave and often darted in amongst flying legs to get in a header. But most of his work was done with his feet – and they were magical at times. Capped by England at under-23 level, Clark seemed destined for full international honours as he produced some sparkling performances on Albion's left wing week in, week out. He scored some cracking goals too, including 12 in 1965/66 when he helped Albion win the League Cup at the first attempt and netted 29 in senior competitions the following season. But, despite scoring in every round and securing a classic first-half brace at Wembley, he still finished up on the losing side in the League Cup final, as West Brom were beaten by his former club QPR.

Clark and Albion returned to the Empire Stadium in 1968 and this time he collected an FA Cup winners' medal after Jeff Astle's extra-time goal had beaten Everton. Injuries then disrupted Clark's performances and, after struggling at times during the course of the 1968/69 campaign, he left The Hawthorns in June 1969 for Preston North End. He later returned to Loftus Road for a second spell before rounding off his career playing, in turn, for Southport, Telford United, in the NASL with Washington Diplomats, Dallas Tornadoes and Philadelphia Fury, and finally Skegness Town in 1977.

Clark now resides in Filey, but is sadly not in good health.

Inside forward/centre forward, 1937-47

Football League:	108	39
FA Cup:	9	4
Other:	96	55
Total:	213	98

Born in the heart of the Black Country (Tipton) in January 1915, Ike Clarke was a fearless, all-action, sturdy centre or inside forward, whose enthusiasm for the game was second to none. He played a lot of intermediate football in the local community and once scored 12 goals in a game for Coseley Juniors, before joining Albion in 1937. He made his Football League debut (*v.* Charlton Athletic) eight months after signing as a professional and was in fine form during the two years before the outbreak of the Second World War, which interrupted his career considerably. Despite this set-back, he still managed to enjoy his football and during the hostilities drew up a fine scoring record with Albion, helping them win the Midland War Cup in 1944.

During the wartime period (1939-46) Clarke was often devastating in and around the penalty area. He was totally committed to playing football and on two occasions went out of his way to serve the Baggies. After a late night out (no explanation was given), he missed his bus, then the tram and also the train! He didn't give up, and cycled twenty miles to Birmingham with his boots strapped to the handlebars to help Albion in a League Cup game. On an earlier occasion he had changed on the bus en route to The Hawthorns and raced down the road, through the door and virtually straight onto the pitch to play in a vital Regional match.

His strike record during the war was tremendous and his best sequence of scoring was in the 1944/45 season, when he bagged a total of 29 goals, including five hat-tricks, one of them being a magnificent effort in a 4-3 win over Aston Villa.

He seemed to figure on the scoresheet every week and that continued the following season when he notched up 19 goals in the Football League South, of which four came in a thumping 8-1 home win over Chelsea.

Always a big favourite amongst The Hawthorns faithful, they were none too pleased when, in 1947, Clarke was sold to Portsmouth by secretary-manager Fred Everiss – at a time when Albion had a very useful forward line comprised of Billy Elliott, Clarke, Irish international Dave Walsh, George Drury and Frank Hodgetts.

Clarke became a star performer in the Pompey attack, helping them to two successive League Championship triumphs (in 1949 and 1950), while scoring 49 goals in 116 games in the process. In 1951, with his senior career coming to an end, he toured Australia with the FA party and played in five 'internationals'. He finished his playing days at Yeovil Town and later managed three Kent sides: Sittingbourne, Canterbury City, and Ashford Town. He retired from the game in 1973 and now resides in the 'Garden of England'.

Jimmy Cookson

Centre forward, 1927-33

Football League:	122	103
FA Cup:	9	7
Total:	131	110

A powerful, all-action centre forward, Jimmy Cookson was a prolific marksman for more than a decade and, in fact, the 100th League goal of his career came in only his 89th match – the quickest individual century of goals from the start of a player's career in football history.

Born in Manchester in December 1904, he played his early football with Clayton FC and Manchester North End before joining Manchester City in 1921. He had a trial with Southport whilst at Maine Road and in 1925 joined Chesterfield, for whom he scored 85 goals in double quick-time; he was top marksman in Division Three (North) in 1925/26. With other clubs keen to sign this ace sharp-shooter, it was Albion who stepped in and brought him to The Hawthorns in June 1927, paying a mere £2,500 for his signature – he immediately started to repay that money with dividends, scoring a double hat-trick as the Baggies whipped Blackpool 6-3 in a Second Division League game three months after he arrived in the Midlands.

He continued to hit the net and went on to claim well over 100 goals in just over 130 appearances for the Baggies, helping them win promotion to the top flight in 1931, the same year he toured Canada with the FA party.

His best season in terms of goals scored was in 1929/30, when he netted 33 in total, all in the League. He weighed in with eleven in the last four games of the season, including two fours, against Hull City and Southampton. He had earlier netted a hat-trick in a 5-0 win over Bradford Park Avenue. He was lethal anywhere around the penalty area and would shoot from any distance, often trying his luck upwards of twenty-five or even thirty yards.

Never a positive header of the ball – he only scored four goals in this manner – Cookson could use both feet (although favouring his right) and he never really slid the ball home, preferring to belt it. He simply had the knack of hitting the target, and whether the goalkeeper saved his shot or not, or the ball struck the woodwork or went into the net, he simply loved shooting!

With Joe Carter, 'W.G.' Richardson and Teddy Sandford all in good form and with a few reserves eagerly awaiting their chance, Cookson – who scored more Second Division goals for Albion than any other player – surprisingly left The Hawthorns in 1933, joining Plymouth Argyle. He later assisted Swindon Town before retiring in 1938 to become a publican.

He stayed in Swindon and recommended Ray Barlow to the Albion in 1944. Cookson died in Warminster in December 1970.

Laurie Cunningham

Winger/inside forward, 1977-79

Football League:	81+5	21
FA Cup:	7+3	3
League Cup:	6	-
Europe:	8	4
Other:	4	2
Total:	106+8	30

Born in East London in March 1956, utility forward Laurie Cunningham was the first black player to represent England in a major international, lining up for this country in an under-21 game against Scotland at Bramall Lane in April 1977 a month after joining West Bromwich Albion. Many thought he would become the first black footballer to win a full England cap. He was, in fact, the second, the first being full-back Viv Anderson.

Cunningham went on to win a further 5 caps at intermediate level, as well as appearing in 6 full internationals and in one 'B' game (in which he came on as a substitute to partner his Hawthorns team-mate Cyrille Regis against Czechoslovakia in Prague in November 1978).

On his day, Cunningham was a brilliant footballer. His electrifying pace, balance and determination, allied to his silky skills on the ball as well as his finishing power, marked him as a truly outstanding talent. He enjoyed playing on the right wing, but during his career occupied every forward position, always performing to an exceptionally high standard.

He had been on Arsenal's books as a junior with Glenn Roeder, but failed to impress the Highbury club. Then George Petchey signed him for Leyton Orient, but admitted: 'There was a time when myself and Peter Angell wondered if we could win him over. He turned up for

training when he liked. But we got there and after nursing him along slowly he became a regular in the side after Barrie Fairbrother was sold to Millwall.'

In 1974/75 he produced some splendid performances for Orient but scored only one goal – a cracker against Southampton – after he had turned up late for the match and was told by assistant manager Petchey that unless he scored he would receive a hefty fine! After an even better 1975/76 campaign, the scouts from the bigger clubs ventured down to Brisbane Road to watch Cunningham in action.

Former West Bromwich Albion and England centre forward Ronnie Allen had monitored his performances with interest while scouting for the Baggies in the London area and he recommended him to player-manager Johnny Giles. Cunningham was transferred to West Bromwich Albion for £110,000 on transfer deadline day in March 1977 in a deal that saw Joe Mayo and Allan Glover move to Orient. Cunningham made an impressive debut for Albion in a 2-0 win at Tottenham a few days after moving to the Midlands, and in 1977/78 played in the FA Cup semi-final defeat by

Ipswich Town.

The following season, under Ron Atkinson's management, he was quite superb at times, helping Albion reach the quarter-finals of the UEFA Cup. One of his finest League displays came on the right wing when full-back Stewart Houston was given a torrid time as Cunningham helped Albion beat Manchester United 5-3 at Old Trafford. He also had a terrific game in Valencia in a UEFA Cup encounter, scoring a fine goal live on Spanish TV.

Real Madrid had been searching for a wide player for twelve months and it came as no surprise, at least not to Albion supporters, when Cunningham was sold to the Spanish giants in the summer of 1979 for a club record incoming fee of almost £1 million. After scoring on his debut for Real in front of 100,000 fans in the Santiago Bernabeau Stadium, he became an overnight hero in Madrid, going on to net 15 goals that season to help his side win the Spanish league and cup double. The following season he collected a runners-up medal when Real lost to Liverpool in the final of the European Cup.

Unfortunately, Cunningham was his own man in Spain. He occasionally missed scheduled training sessions and spent a lot of time as a male model, fashion designer and boutique owner. Repeated absences from the training ground brought on niggling injuries and this led to his eventual departure from Real Madrid, having been on loan to Manchester United and Sporting Gijon whilst registered with the Spanish club. He drifted from club to club afterwards, serving with Olympique Marseille, Leicester City, Rayo Vallecano (two spells), FC Charleroi (Belgium) and Wimbledon. In fact, he won an FA Cup winners' medal with the Dons, coming on as a second-half substitute when they caused a major shock by beating Liverpool 1-0 in the 1988 Cup final.

After that Wembley triumph he returned to Spain to join Second Division side Rayo Vallecano of Madrid and helped them win promotion in his first season. Things seemed to be picking up again for the thirty-three year-old Cunningham but tragically, in the early hours of 15 July 1989, he was killed in a car crash on the outskirts of Madrid.

In an excellent playing career (with every club he served and, indeed, his country) Cunningham appeared in almost 350 competitive games and scored 50 goals. He graced all the big stadiums in Europe and produced some wonderful performances, none better than the one against Valencia in Spain when Albion drew 1-1 in the UEFA Cup in 1978 and that terrific 5-3 League win by the Baggies at Old Trafford that same year.

Stan Davies

Inside forward/centre forward, 1921-27

Football League:	147	77
FA Cup:	12	6
Total:	159	83

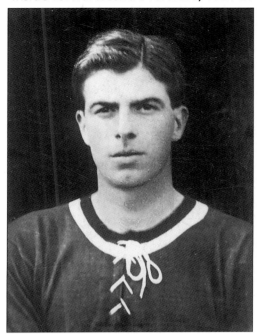

The versatile Stan Davies could play in any position, even as a goalkeeper. He was a tremendous footballer, but it was as an inside or centre forward where he did the most damage. A Welshman, born in Chirk in April 1898, he had been in football for six years before joining West Bromwich Albion from Everton in November 1921 for £3,300. He went straight into the first team (against Manchester City, at home) and quickly formed a fine strike force with Fred Morris. He top-scored with 17 League and cup goals in his first season at The Hawthorns and in 1922/23 he netted another 21, ably assisted by Morris in both instances. Injuries interrupted his progress between 1923 and 1925 but he bounced back in style during the 1925/26 campaign with 19 goals from playing up front with George James and Charlie 'Tug' Wilson.

Davies had another excellent season after that but then lost his place in the side to Jimmy Cookson, and this led to him leaving The Hawthorns to join neighbouring Birmingham for £1,500.

Prior to teaming up with Everton in January 1921, Davies had worked down the coal mines in mid-Wales for twelve months before joining the local football team, Chirk, keeping goal for the Second XI in the Oswestry & District League.

When war broke out, Davies joined the Volunteers in Aberystwyth and was immediately sent for combat training. By November 1914 he found himself in France serving with the Welsh Fusiliers on the Western Front. He was wounded at Cambrai and when he was discharged from hospital he joined the Army Signalling School in Dunstable. Davies ended the war with the Military Medal and the Belgian Croix de Guerre. He resumed playing football straight after the war, and had a trial with Manchester United before joining Rochdale.

He switched to Preston North End and then moved on to Everton for £4,000 in January 1921. He averaged a goal every two games over his Albion career and then netted 5 times in his 17 outings for Blues before moving to Cardiff City in May 1928.

Thereafter he was player-manager of Rotherham United, served briefly with Barnsley, Manchester Central, Dudley Town, Chelmsford City (as player-trainer) and was manager of the Rochester-based Shorts FC before quitting football in 1945 at the age of forty-seven.

He played in 18 full internationals and one 'other' game for Wales, occupying six different positions. Stan died in Birmingham in January 1972.

Jimmy Dudley

Inside right/right-half, 1944-59

Football League:	285	9
FA Cup:	34	2
Other:	1	-
Total:	320	11

Originally an inside forward, Jimmy Dudley developed into a very professional and competent right-half who played the game diligently, without ever being extravagent. He was a methodical footballer, who was very rarely cautioned, and created an Albion club record of 166 consecutive League appearances over a four-year period (1952-56). This stood for twenty-three years, until it was beaten by defender Ally Robertson in 1979.

Dudley, who was born in Gartcosh, Glasgow in August 1928, was the workhorse in the midfield and provided the vital link between defence and attack, a job he did manfully, not only for Albion but also for Walsall whom he helped gain promotion from the Fourth to the Second Division in successive seasons. He joined Albion from the Albright Youth Club in August 1944 and turned professional twelve months later. He graduated through the ranks at The Hawthorns and formed part of two splendid Baggies' half-back lines – the first comprising Jimmy Dugdale in the centre half berth and Ray Barlow to his left, and the second featuring the raven-haired Joe Kennedy in the centre half position.

Dudley began to show his pedigree during the 1950/51 season, when he was called into action either as a right half or inside right in sixteen League games. He scored one goal, a real gem against Derby County. The following season he again filled both of those berths before settling down in the number four shirt, which he retained, with confidence and reliability, until the arrival of the bandy-legged Devon-born Maurice Setters. Even then Dudley, under pressure at times, still produced the goods and it wasn't until halfway through the 1958/59 campaign that he finally dropped into the reserves on a permanent basis.

Dudley was eventually replaced at right half at The Hawthorns by Maurice Setters in 1957 – three years after he had gained an FA Cup winners' medal when Albion defeated Preston 3-2 in the final. It was Dudley who scored his side's equalising goal against Port Vale in the semi-final – certainly the most important one of the few he netted for the club at senior level (in more than 300 appearances).

Dudley, who was capped by Scotland at 'B' team level (*v*. England in 1954), left Albion in 1959. He went on to appear in 176 League and cup games for Walsall and, after announcing his retirement from football in 1964, he worked in the spares department of Guest Motors in West Bromwich for eighteen years.

Jimmy's brother, George Dudley, was an Albion player from 1937 to 1946. Their cousin was the 1930s Baggies stalwart Jimmy 'Iron' Edwards.

Jimmy Dugdale
Centre half, 1952-56

Football League:	63	-
FA Cup:	11	-
Other:	0+1	-
Total:	94+1	-

Born in Liverpool in January 1932, centre half Jimmy Dugdale made an impressive senior debut for West Bromwich Albion by completely blotting out the threat of England's Nat Lofthouse, who had already scored five international goals that season as well as seven for Bolton Wanderers.

After that positive performance against the player dubbed 'The Lion of Vienna', Dugdale grew in confidence and stature and produced some excellent displays in the Central League side.

He was engaged in first-team action again in February 1953 and was a regular in the Albion side for the last third of that season. He then played his heart out in 1953/54 as the Baggies – rated as the best footballing unit in the country – came so near to becoming the first team in the twentieth century to win the League and FA Cup double. They finished runners-up to Wolves in the First Division, but beat Preston to win the FA Cup.

Dugdale played in thirty-two of the forty-two League games that season, but only managed thirteen outings the following term and just three in 1955/56. He was sold for what seemed a rather moderate £25,000 in a move that surprised many Albion supporters.

Unfortunately for Dugdale, the Baggies had another tremendous centre half on their books at the same time, Joe Kennedy, and with Aston Villa eager to find a replacement for Irish international Con Martin, manager Vic Buckingham reluctantly agreed to transfer Jimmy to their arch-rivals.

A year after leaving The Hawthorns, Dugdale added a second FA Cup winners medal to his collection, having by now bedded himself into Villa's defence alongside Pat Saward.

He played the game with aggression and power and missed very few first team games between 1956 and 1961. He helped Villa regain their First Division status and become the winners of the first ever Football League Cup final.

After making more than 250 appearances for Villa, Dugdale ended his career in London with QPR, injury forcing him into early retirement in 1962 when he moved into the licensing trade. In later life he had to have a leg amputated and he is now confined to a wheelchair. His uncle was the former Coventry City, Charlton Athletic and Barnsley defender Alan Dugdale.

Jimmy Edwards

Inside left/left-half, 1926-37

Football League:	182	9
FA Cup:	19	-
Other:	1	-
Total:	202	9

After commencing his professional career as a go-ahead, all-action inside left, Jimmy 'Iron' Edwards was successfully converted into a rock-solid, resolute and indefatigable left-half, who gave Albion splendid service for over ten years. Born in Tipton in December 1905, he had two 'breaking in' spells with Stourbridge before joining Albion's professional staff in May 1926.

He made his senior debut in the Second Division game against Hull City at Boothferry Park in March 1928, and after that he went from strength to strength as he accumulated over 200 first-team appearances for the Baggies. He was a key member of the side that completed the unique double in 1930/31 (victory in the FA Cup final and promotion to the top flight in the same season). He also played in the 1935 Cup Final defeat and represented the Football League.

With his tree-trunk legs, solid hips, biting tackle and determination, Edwards was the anchorman in the centre of the field, playing alongside centre half Bill Richardson (the pair were called 'Iron and Steel') and behind Teddy Sandford and winger Stan Wood. A competitive footballer, always alert and never found wanting, he eventually lost his place in the team during the 1935/36 campaign when Jack Sankey and Jack Rix were challenging strongly for selection. He eventually left The Hawthorns for Norwich City in May 1937.

Edwards, well liked and admired by the supporters for his tireless endeavour and totally committed performances, suffered with injuries during the 1931/32 and 1932/33 seasons, but he manfully fought his way back to full fitness and never let the side down, even when he was not fully fit.

He acted as skipper from time to time and was always aiding and abetting the younger players in the team. Even when sidelined, he was a great asset to the reserves, passing on some of his vast experience to those who were to be future players for the club.

One of those he advised was Sammy Heaselgrave, whom he took under his wing. Heaselgrave made Albion's first team, but the war seriously disrupted his progress. Edwards believed he would have become an England international.

Edwards later assisted Bilston United, Kingswinford and Dudley Town before announcing his retirement in 1944.

Edwards, whose brother Ernie also played for Albion (1913-14), died in West Bromwich in April 1982.

Billy Elliott
Outside right, 1938-52

Football League:	170	39
FA Cup:	12	1
Other:	148	117
Total:	330	157

Billy Elliott was a stocky, fast-raiding outside right who displayed splendid close ball control, plenty of tricks (some them extremely cunning), a cracking right-foot shot and a penchant for hard work.

Born in Harrington, Cumberland in August 1919, he played briefly for Carlisle United, Wolverhampton Wanderers and Bournemouth before joining Albion for £4,000 in December 1938, making his debut for the club almost immediately against Luton Town.

The Second World War failed to disrupt his career. Indeed, he was a star performer throughout the hostilities, scoring over 100 goals in almost 150 Regional League and cup appearances and he also gained 2 England Victory international caps (it would have been far more if a certain Stanley Matthews hadn't been around).

His best scoring campaign in fact came in wartime – 1941/42 – when he netted 31 times. He found the net in ten successive Regional games between 20 September and 6 December and his haul included a hat-trick in a terrific 8-2 victory at Wolves.

His best scoring performance either side of the 1939-45 wartime period was in 1946/47, when he notched up 10 in the Second Division, but he certainly laid on plenty of chances for his colleagues, as he did again in 1947/48 and 1948/49 with Dave Walsh the main beneficiary. He admitted: 'I loved to see Billy racing down the wing – I knew he would get in a cross sooner or later. I just had to make sure I could get there in time!'

Elliott – who was a integral part of Albion's Second Division promotion-winning side in 1948/49 – loved to hug the touchline and he often bemused his opponent (sometimes even causing the hapless defender to stop) by drawing his foot over the ball while dashing down the wing. A firm favourite with the fans, he always seemed to find space inside the penalty area, especially when the ball was on the opposite flank, hence his excellent goal-tally.

An Achilles tendon injury (suffered against Wolves at Molineux in April 1951) effectively ended Elliott's League career. He left The Hawthorns shortly before the start of the next season and soon afterwards became player-manager of Bilston United, retiring in 1954 when he became landlord of the Farcroft Hotel in Handsworth.

Elliott died whilst on holiday in the Canary Islands in November 1966.

Bob Finch

Full-back, 1925-39

Football League:	216	-
FA Cup:	18	-
Total:	234	-

Bob Finch was a redoubtable full-back. Safe, reliable and cool under pressure, he was an excellent club man who, for many years, skippered West Bromwich Albion's second team after failing to dislodge George Shaw and Bert Trentham from the full-back positions in the first team.

Born in Hednesford, deep in coal-mining country, in August 1908, he joined Albion from his hometown club, Hednesford Town, in April 1925 and made his League debut six months later against Leicester City – the first of more than 230 senior appearances for the Baggies.

Finch gained a regular first-team place soon after the start of the 1927/28 season (after Bill Ashurst had departed and Dicky Baugh had been injured).

He retained the right-back berth until losing his place in September 1930 when Shaw and Trentham were installed as defensive partners in front of goalkeeper Harold Pearson. As Albion stormed through to claim the double of FA Cup glory and promotion, Finch languished in the reserves, only occasionally filtering into the First XI.

He was, however, a valuable member of the squad and never let the side down when called into action. He came back in the mid-1930s and starred in Albion's epic 3-1 FA Cup home win over Arsenal – when a record 64,815 crowd assembled at The Hawthorns – but was then a disappointed man when the team lost to Preston in the semi-final showdown at Highbury.

That cup-tie against the Gunners took place in 1936/37 season, when Finch lined up at right-back with new signing Cecil Shaw (from Wolves) joining him halfway through the campaign following the injury to and eventual demotion of Bert Trentham. Finch held firm for most of the following season before being replaced in the side by Harold White. Finch's last senior outing was against Blackpool at Bloomfield Road in April 1938, when he had a rather poor game as Albion, fighting in vain against relegation, lost 2-1.

Another spell in the reserves followed and he took his Second XI appearance tally to well past the 230 mark. He had earlier gained three successive Central League championship medals, and had captained the side in two of the three campaigns. Finch left Albion for Swansea Town in May 1939 after fourteen years at The Hawthorns. Unfortunately, the war meant that his days of competitive playing were virtually over. He later returned to his former club Hednesford Town (albeit only briefly) and served in the Staffordshire police force until 1956. Finch was also an active member of the local golf club and he was seen on the golf course until well into his nineties. Finch died at Hednesford in December 2000.

Doug Fraser

Football League:	255+2	8
FA Cup:	24	-
League Cup:	29	4
Europe:	10	-
Other:	5	-
Total:	323+2	12

Doug Fraser was born in Busby, Lanarkshire in February 1941 and, after trials with Celtic and Leeds United, he joined Aberdeen as a professional on his seventeenth birthday. A gritty performer, though not without style, he played as an attacking wing-half for the first ten years of his senior career before starring as a hard-tackling, sure-footed right-back during his last three years with West Bromwich Albion. He occupied a more central defensive position with both Nottingham Forest and Walsall, but was also called on to play at left-back.

Fraser left his native Scotland to join West Bromwich Albion in 1963 after almost 90 appearances for the Dons. He made his Albion debut against Birmingham City in a home First Division fixture on 18 September 1963.

At The Hawthorns, Fraser initially played in front of England international right-back Don Howe and behind winger Kenny Foggo. The trio did well together, with Fraser also a key figure in the Baggies' midfield, where he accompanied fellow Scot Bobby Hope. A vital part of Albion's League Cup and FA Cup-winning sides in the late 1960s, Fraser also played in the 1967 and 1970 League Cup finals, skippering Albion against Manchester City in the latter.

In November 1970, Fraser was injured playing against Chelsea. He struggled to regain full fitness and two months later (after being replaced at full-back by Graham Lovett) he was transferred to Nottingham Forest, having appeared in well over 300 games for Albion. He also won his 2 Scottish caps whilst at The Hawthorns (*v.* Holland and Cyprus in the late 1960s) and toured Australia with his country in 1967.

With Forest, where he played alongside another former West Brom star, Ronnie Rees, Fraser missed only 9 League games out of a possible 94 before being sold by manager Dave Mackay to Walsall. In January 1974, he became player-manager at Fellows Park, a position he held for over three years. During that time the Saddlers were consistently a mid-table Third Division side, although they did reach the fifth round of the FA Cup in 1975.

Fraser quit football in 1977 to enter the prison service, and worked at Nottingham Prison until his retirement through ill health in 1994.

Johnny Giles
Midfielder, 1975-77

Football League:	74+1	3
FA Cup:	4	-
League Cup:	4	1
Other:	5	1
Total:	87+1	5

Recovering well from a broken leg, suffered at the outset of his professional life as a footballer with Manchester United, Johnny Giles became a brilliant midfield schemer whose career spanned almost thirty years. Born in Dublin in November 1940, he joined the groundstaff at Old Trafford in 1956 and, after 114 appearances for the Reds, and with an FA Cup winners' medal to his name, he moved to Elland Road for £37,500 in 1963. Over the next twelve years he won honours galore under Don Revie's management and scored 115 goals in 524 matches for Leeds, before becoming West Bromwich Albion's first-ever player-manager, being appointed in June 1975.

In his initial season at The Hawthorns, he transformed Albion from a moderate, and sometimes struggling, Second Division side, into a promotion-winning outfit. He recruited some fine players – fellow countrymen Paddy Mulligan and Mick Martin among them – and his midfielder generalship shone through as Albion matched and beat some of the best teams in the country. Able to dictate play with his intelligent passing, Giles got the best out of the average player and he did a great deal in helping

the Baggies consolidate their position in top flight, his experience and presence being much appreciated by the team and, indeed, the supporters.

He ran the midfield engine room and his vast experience and knowledge of the game certainly rubbed off on players like Len Cantello, the young Bryan Robson and Laurie Cunningham, whom he signed from Leyton Orient.

Giles, a predominantly right-footed player, could turn a game with one single flash of brilliance. He scored some cracking goals, while also laying on chances aplenty for his colleagues.

It was a pity he didn't arrive at The Hawthorns three or four years earlier. Who knows what might have happened …

Giles chose to leave The Hawthorns after two seasons, moving back 'home' to take over as player-manager of Shamrock Rovers, later becoming executive director of that club. In January 1978 he switched to the NASL with Philadelphia Fury, taking over as coach of Vancouver Whitecaps in November 1980 only to return for a second spell as boss at The Hawthorns in February 1984, holding office for seventeen months before pulling out of football. Capped 60 times by the Republic of Ireland, he appeared in 5 FA Cup finals, equalling the pre-war record set by Joe Hulme of Huddersfield Town and Arsenal. The brother-in-law of Nobby Stiles, Giles became a soccer journalist and also worked for Irish television.

Johnny Giles in action for Albion against his former club Leeds United and one-time team-mate Allan Clarke on the opening day of the 1976/77 League season at Elland Road. The game ended in a 2-2 draw.

Tommy Glidden
Outside-right, 1921-36

Football League:	445	135
FA Cup:	33	5
Other:	1	-
Total:	479	140

As a youngster Tommy Glidden played in every forward position, before finally settling down as a goalscoring right-winger who skippered Albion in two FA Cup finals (1931 and 1935). A very nimble footballer, he had excellent ball control, good pace and a strong shot, he was a key member of the Baggies' side for twelve years before a knee injury forced him into retirement.

Born in Coxlodge, Newcastle-upon-Tyne in July 1902, he joined the professional staff at The Hawthorns (from Sunderland Albion) in April 1922, having been an amateur with Sunderland and a trialist with Bristol City prior to that. He made his League debut at Everton in November 1922 and, after a brief spell on the left flank and a season in the reserves, he became a regular in the first team in 1924/25, when he took over at outside right from Jimmy Spencer. Positive in his style and approach, Glidden linked up superbly with Joe Carter and Tommy Magee as Albion completed the double in 1930/31.

With his decisive and pin-point crosses (which he was capable of delivering at speed) he created plenty of goals for centre forwards Jimmy Cookson (initially) and then 'W.G.' Richardson, as well as regularly scoring himself: he grabbed 140 goals in almost 480 senior appearances for the Baggies – a splendid return for a winger.

His best scoring season was in 1927/28, when he netted 21 goals in 40 League games. He claimed a hat-trick in a 5-2 win at Chelsea, in what was one of Albion's best displays of the campaign, and he was instrumental in other big victories over Swansea Town (when he helped set up three of the five goals), Barnsley and Reading, scoring twice against the Tykes.

Glidden would often cut in from his wing position and find a spot just inside the penalty area. Most of his goals came from the right side of the box, although he did net a match-winning long-range effort against Everton in the FA Cup semi-final at Old Trafford in March 1931 – undoubtedly his most important strike in an Albion shirt!

Glidden, who represented England schoolboys in 1914 and figured in an international trial in 1925/26, hung up his boots in the summer of 1936 and immediately became a coach at The Hawthorns, a position he held for three years. In 1951 he returned to the club as a director, holding office until his death in West Bromwich in July 1974.

Tony Godden
Goalkeeper, 1975-85

Football League:	267	-
FA Cup:	19	-
League Cup:	27	-
Europe:	12	-
Other:	4	-
Total:	329	-

On his day Tony Godden was a fine goalkeeper – positive, a good shot-stopper and confident with crosses. Born in Gillingham in August 1955, and educated locally, he was an amateur at the Priestfield Stadium before joining Ashford Town, from where he switched to The Hawthorns for £5,000 in August 1975 (after a trial at Molineux).

One of Johnny Giles' first recruits, it was the Irishman who gave Godden his League debut at Tottenham in March 1977 (the same day that Laurie Cunningham first appeared in a Baggies shirt). He did well, helping Albion to a 2-0 victory. After that, Godden produced many excellent performances, often keeping Albion in a game they would have normally lost hands down. He saved a handful of vital penalties – one at Molineux helped send Wolves into the Second Division, while another twelve yard stop went a long way to earning Albion a splendid League Cup win at Everton.

He was a sound 'keeper but he did have lapses of concentration, and once even allowed Liverpool's Kenny Dalglish to creep up from behind and score a goal at The Hawthorns!

In his first two years with Albion, he understudied John Osborne and was also loaned to Preston. Thereafter he did very well and appeared in over 320 games for the Baggies (228 consecutively up to October 1981). He had a game with Happy Valley FC (Hong Kong) before signing for Chelsea in May 1986, after an earlier loan spell at Stamford Bridge, as well as a similar period at Walsall. In August 1987, the Blues acquired Godden's services, paying Albion £35,000 for the player. In August 1989 he went to Peterborough United, following further loan spells with Bury (December 1988) and Sheffield Wednesday (March and April 1989), and in July 1990 he dropped out of League football to sign for Wivenhoe Town, returning briefly as a loan player with Colchester United in March 1991.

After retiring as a player, he managed Warboys Town (from August 1991), was registered with March Town, then managed Kings Lynn (from May 1994), Bury Town (from May 1996) and Wisbech Town as well as acting as coach with Rushden & Diamonds, Notts County, Northampton Town and Peterborough United (his current club at the time of writing in 2001).

Don Goodman

Striker, 1986-91

Football League:	140+18	60
FA Cup:	7	1
League Cup:	11	1
Other:	5	1
Total:	163+18	63

A Yorkshireman born in Leeds in May 1966, Don Goodman played as a junior for Collingham FC before signing professional forms for Bradford City in July 1984. An aggressive, pacy, all-action striker, he went on to score over 20 goals for the Bantams and was at Valley Parade at the time of the Bradford fire disaster in 1985. In March 1987 he joined West Bromwich Albion for £50,000 and he did extremely well at The Hawthorns, scoring some memorable goals for the Baggies.

Sometimes asked to be the lone striker, grafting away without a single complaint, he was admired by the fans, although in his first full season at the club he struggled to find the net. Thereafter, however, he found scoring comfortable and in 1988/89, when he was ably assisted by first Gary Robson and then by Kevin Bartlett, he bagged 15 in the League (including 3 in the home game with Crystal Palace – his first hat-trick for Albion). Despite playing in a team which was struggling at times, Goodman battled on regardless, putting in some sterling performances, especially in 1989/90 when he weighed in with another 21 League goals,

including his second hat-trick, this time in an emphatic 7-0 home win over Barnsley.

In December 1991, Sunderland secured his services for £900,000 – much to the annoyance of all Baggies' fans. At Roker Park he continued to find the net and hit 44 goals in more than 130 outings before his £1.1 million transfer to Wolves in December 1994. His playing career almost came to an end when he suffered a depressed fracture of the skull when performing in the Wanderers' penultimate League game of the 1995/96 season against Huddersfield Town.

Thankfully, after some nervous moments and several hours of medical care and attention, he recovered to full fitness and went on to serve the club until the summer of 1998, when he was released to join the Japaneze J-League side Hiroshima. He later teamed up with Scottish club Motherwell (after a brief spell with Barnsley), and in March 2001 returned to the West Midlands to sign for promotion-chasing Walsall.

He did very well for the Saddlers as Ray Graydon's team pushed hard for promotion from Division Two. He scored some vital goals, none more so than the one he plundered in the play-off final at Cardiff's Millennium Stadium to set Walsall on their way to an excellent victory over Reading as they regained their place in the Nationwide League Division One at the first attempt.

Football League:	162	39
FA Cup:	13	3
Other:	6	3
Total:	181	45

West Bromwich Albion's left-wing partnership of Fred Morris and Howard Gregory was one of the finest at club level anywhere in the country from 1919 until 1923. Indeed, the two players were in tremendous form during the first full season after the First World War when the First Division Championship came to The Hawthorns. They scored almost 50 goals between them, Gregory contributing 12.

The ginger-haired Gregory, who was fast and direct, was a winger of the highest quality who could score goals as well as make them.

Born in rival territory at Aston Manor, Birmingham in May 1894, he joined Albion on his seventeenth birthday, having played local football for two years. He made his senior debut against Everton in April 1912, gained a regular place in Albion's first team in 1919 (when he took over the left-wing duties from Ben Shearman) and played his last senior game for the Baggies in March 1925, having handed over his shirt to Jack Byers.

During the period from 1919-25, when Albion were a powerful attacking side which was scoring plenty of goals, Gregory was regularly fed from behind by the strong-limbed Bobby McNeal. Often McNeal would race away down the wing before the ball was delivered by the left-half; it would often land right in front of the flying Gregory as he dashed towards the touchline before attempting to fire over a telling centre, hit high or low for his strikers.

Gregory enjoyed a competitive battle and often challenged the heavier defenders with grim determination, never pulling out of a 50-50 situation. He was an aggressive player at times, but always managed to control his temper and never received a caution or even a stern lecture.

Nicknamed the 'Express Man', Gregory once struck a soaking wet, leather football so hard during a game against Wolverhampton Wanderers at Molineux that the casing split before it reached the goal, the bladder flying over the bar and the casing into the net!

He was forced to retire through injury at the end of the 1925/26 season, having scored, on average, one goal in every four games for Albion.

Gregory was the licensee of the Woodman Inn (next to The Hawthorns) for five years (1927-32) and remained in that line of business until the early 1950s. He died in August 1954 at the age of sixty.

Frank Griffin

Outside right, 1950-58

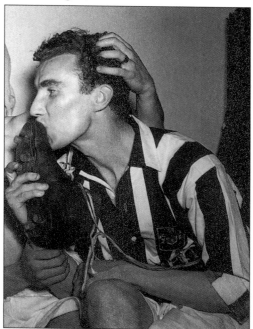

Football League:	240	47
FA Cup:	34	5
Other:	1	-
Total:	275	52

Born in Pendlebury, Manchester in March 1928, fast-raiding outside right Frank Griffin had been a trialist with Hull City and an amateur with Bolton Wanderers before breaking into League football with Shrewsbury Town. He quickly brought scouts flooding to the Gay Meadow ground and it was no surprise when West Bromwich Albion secured his services towards the end of the 1951/52 season as a replacement for the badly injured Billy Elliott.

Ronnie Allen had been playing on the right wing following his arrival from Port Vale, but Albion wanted to move him into the middle and left the door open for Griffin to make his name. He went on to give the Baggies tremendous service until a broken leg disrupted his career. A player who loved to hug the touchline, Griffin had both speed and skill, and he also packed a fierce right-foot shot when he chose to have a crack at goal.

An expert at taking corner-kicks, Griffin laid on three goals from the flag for Ronnie Allen in a tremendous 5-2 home win over Chelsea in 1953 and soon afterwards had a hand in three more when Cardiff City were clipped 6-1, again at The Hawthorns. He also netted a fine individual goal at Wolves in an FA Cup-tie. He very rarely switched wings but when he ventured inside he claimed a handful of goals.

A positive footballer, never afraid to take on the burly full-backs, Griffin enjoyed a challenge.

In 1954 he scored a dramatic 87th minute goal to bring Albion victory over Preston North End in the FA Cup final, and three years later he netted the only hat-trick of his career when the Baggies crushed Manchester City's 'M' plan to the tune of 9-2 in a First Division League match at The Hawthorns.

Although he had both Stanley Matthews (Blackpool) and Tom Finney (Preston) plus a few more outside rights to contend with, Griffin was in line to win his first representative honour in February 1958 – but it was not to be. Sadly, his right leg was broken in a crunching tackle by Sheffield United defender Joe Shaw in a fifth round FA Cup replay. He never really recovered from that mishap and, although he battled on and played in three more League games during the second half of the 1958/59 season, he was never quite the same.

With young Jimmy Campbell already showing good form on the right wing, Griffin was transferred to Northampton Town, where he spent the last season of his senior career. He had brief spells with Wellington Town and then GKN Sankey FC, before announcing his retirement in 1965, when he took over as manager of non-League Worthern United. Griffin later lived and worked in Shrewsbury.

Asa Hartford

Midfielder, 1966-74

Football League:	206+9	18
FA Cup:	19	2
League Cup:	15	2
Europe:	6	3
Other:	20	1
Total:	266+9	26

Scottish international midfielder Asa Hartford will perhaps always be remembered as the player whose transfer to the then First Division giants Leeds United was sensationally called off at the eleventh hour after a routine medical check had revealed a hole-in-the-heart condition. This was in November 1971, when the blond-haired Hartford was poised to leave West Bromwich Albion for Elland Road in a deal worth £170,000. Hartford's condition, happily, turned out to be only a minor one. In August 1974, after Albion had failed to regain their First Division status following relegation in 1973, he moved to Manchester City for £225,000.

Hartford, who was named Asa after the famous American singer Al Jolson, was born in Clydebank in October 1950 and joined Albion as a youngster in 1966, turning professional in October 1967. He was a dynamic footballer, covering acres of ground every time he played a match. Full of energy, with his stamina never a problem, he was an industrious, all-action competitive engine-room grafter, always buzzing around, seeking an opening and creating chances aplenty for his colleagues as well as scoring a few goals himself. He linked up exceedingly well with Len Cantello and Bobby Hope in Albion's midfield and later aided and abetted some of the finest footballers in the land as his career expanded.

He appeared in 275 first-class games for Albion, gaining a League Cup runners-up prize in 1970 – he collected a winners' medal in the same competition with Manchester City in 1976 and won a third with Norwich City in 1985 (when his deflected shot decided the game with Sunderland). Between these occasions he played for Nottingham Forest (briefly in July and August 1979), Everton (1979-81), Manchester City (for a second spell from 1981-84) and Fort Lauderdale Sun (NASL).

After leaving Carrow Road he moved to Bolton Wanderers and later assisted Stockport County (as a player and manager, 1987-89), Oldham Athletic (1989) and finally Shrewsbury Town before taking up coaching, initially at Blackburn, followed by Stoke City and then at his old club Manchester City. Capped 50 times by Scotland, Hartford also represented his country at youth, Under 21 and Under 23 levels and, when he hung up his boots in 1991, he had amassed in excess of 800 games in all competitions; he was, in short, a very fine footballer.

Norman Heath

Goalkeeper, 1942-55

Football League:	121	-
FA Cup:	13	-
Other:	35	-
Total:	169	-

West Bromwich Albion's agile and courageous goalkeeper Norman Heath was all set to appear in the 1954 FA Cup final against Preston North End, but a month before the big event he was badly injured whilst playing in a re-arranged First Division League game at Roker Park. He dived at the feet of Ted Purdon, Sunderland's South African-born centre forward and severely damaged his neck and spine, suffering paralysis from the waist down. Sadly, he spent the rest of his life in a wheelchair.

In competition with Tommy Grimley and Jimmy Sanders, he had worked hard to claim his first team place at The Hawthorns, but with his sights set on Wembley he and the Baggies were dealt a shuddering blow.

Heath had made his first team debut for the club during the Second World War but when Sanders arrived from Charlton Athletic in 1945 he went back into the reserves.

He got back into the first team during the second half of the 1947/48 campaign and actually began his League career in style by saving a penalty on his debut against Sheffield Wednesday at Hillsborough twelve days before Christmas in 1947.

He then lost out again (to Sanders) when Albion gained promotion to the top flight the following season but he always produced the goods, playing exceedingly well in the Second XI, ready and eager to win back his first team place.

After a long process of competitiveness between himself and Sanders, Heath got back into the senior side halfway through the 1951/52 season and remained the first choice 'keeper until that incident in the north-east.

Born in Wolverhampton in January 1924, Heath had represented Wolverhampton Boys and was spotted by Albion while keeping goal for Henry Meadows FC. He was signed in May 1942, turned professional in October 1943 and slowly graduated through the junior ranks with Albion, playing in several wartime matches. He was a well built 'keeper who never lacked confidence. He was commanding and authoritative behind full-backs Stan Rickaby and skipper Len Millard and half-backs Jimmy Dudley, Jimmy Dugdale (or Joe Kennedy) and Ray Barlow for two seasons before that devastating injury on Wearside.

In later life Heath lived and worked in Birmingham before his death at Great Barr in November 1983.

Football League:	331+5	33
FA Cup:	19	-
League Cup:	29	7
Europe:	9	1
Other:	10	1
Total:	398+5	42

Bobby Hope was a player who displayed masterly qualities in midfield. At his zenith nobody bettered him at passing, either in thought or in accuracy. His excellent ball skills and defence-splitting through balls were highlights of a wonderful association with West Bromwich Albion.

There is no doubt that he 'made' the career of outside left Clive Clark, feeding the dashing winger whenever he could with short and long passes. He linked up splendidly with fellow midfielders Doug Fraser, Ian Collard, Graham Lovett and, finally, Asa Hartford and Len Cantello, and he provided plenty of ammunition for strikers Jeff Astle, Tony Brown and John Kaye (before the latter became a defender).

Born in Bridge of Allan, Stirlingshire in September 1943, Hope was signed as a fifteen-year-old by Baggies manager Gordon Clark with fellow Scots Campbell Crawford, Kenny Foggo and Bobby Murray, three months after all four players had starred for Scotland schoolboys against England. He developed quickly and was given his senior baptism before he had turned professional, becoming Albion's youngest League debutant since Charlie Wilson in October 1921. That game, a First Division home encounter with Arsenal on 30 April 1960, was the first of more than 400 competitive games for Albion, with whom he won both League Cup and FA Cup winners' medals. He also played in the 1967 and 1970 losing League Cup final sides and had the distinction of scoring Albion's first goal in a major European competition, against DOS Utrecht in a Fairs Cup encounter in Holland in November 1966. He gained his 2 full caps whilst at The Hawthorns, playing against Holland and Denmark in 1968 and 1969. He deserved more and would undoubtedly have earned further recognition if he had been with a bigger club!

A fine striker of the ball, Hope scored some cracking goals in his time. He fired home a rasping twenty-five yard drive against Tottenham Hotspur at The Hawthorns in May 1966 and followed this with another against Arsenal at Highbury five months later. He also netted two stunning efforts when claiming his only first-class hat-trick for Albion as they whipped rivals Aston Villa 6-1 in a League Cup-tie in between those two matches against the North London clubs.

Bobby Hope receiving treatment from Albion trainer Wilf Dixon during the home League game with Leicester City in August 1963.

In 1972 Hope was a surprise signing by Birmingham City manager Freddie Goodwin, who was looking to boost his newly-promoted squad. After a bright enough start he struggled at St Andrew's and eventually elected to join the exodus to America, where he assisted Philadelphia Atoms and Dallas Tornadoes, before returning to England to have a brief flirtation with Sheffield Wednesday.

In August 1978 Hope began a five-year association with Bromsgrove Rovers, initially as player-manager. He was in charge of Burton Albion in 1988 and returned for a second spell with Bromsgrove in 1989.

Ten years later he was back at The Hawthorns, working as the club's youth development scout before being officially appointed as the club's chief scout (November 2000) as Richie Barker's successor. Hope also ran post offices in Birmingham and Sutton Coldfield during the 1980s.

Football League:	47	-
FA Cup:	36	1
Total:	83	1

Nicknamed 'Ironsides', Ezra Horton was a solid, uncompromising, hard-tackling and totally committed right-half. He played in three consecutive FA Cup finals with Albion, being on the losing side in 1886 against Blackburn Rovers and in 1887 versus Aston Villa, before lifting the trophy at Preston North End's expense in 1888. In this game he was outstanding behind Albion's excellent right-wing pairing of Billy Bassett and George 'Spry' Woodhall.

A local man, born in West Bromwich in August 1861, Horton played for the George Salter works team and for West Bromwich FC before joining Albion in August 1882, turning professional three years later. He quickly established himself in the side and went on to amass a fine record of more than 300 appearances in various League, cup and friendly matches during his nine years with the club. He played in Albion's first-ever FA Cup-tie (*v.* Wednesbury Town in 1883) and in the club's first-ever League game (*v.* Stoke in 1888) – being one of only two players to do so.

He was a very consistent performer and always gave 100 per cent out on the field. His sleeves were frequently rolled up to the elbow, his hair was greased and he certainly looked an aggressive, all-action footballer – which he was, although Horton was very rarely in trouble with the referees. He played the game hard but fair. An ever-present in 1889/90, his only goal for the club was against Wednesbury Old Athletic in a first round FA Cup tie in October 1887: he struck it with venom in a convincing 7-1 victory. But scoring goals was not his forte – although he helped make them while trying to prevent the opposition from scoring at the other end of the field.

He began to suffer a few injuries during the 1890/91 season, dislocating his toe twice and his elbow once – he even played on with a cracked wrist. But Horton simply loved playing football and he was perhaps somewhat disappointed when he finally called it a day!

In June 1891, with his brother Jack still registered as a player with the club, he announced his retirement and soon afterwards became a football referee.

He died in West Bromwich in July 1939. Horton had, in fact, been a guest player for Aston Villa in 1884/85 and he also played for England in a hockey international *v.* Ireland in 1898, becoming only the second West Midlander at that time to win such an honour in the sport.

Don Howe

Right-back, 1949-64

Football League:	342	17
FA Cup:	37	2
Total:	379	19

Deft positioning, reliability, strength, powerful kicking and general acumen were the hallmarks of Don Howe's performances at right-back for both West Bromwich Albion and England. During his later years at The Hawthorns, Howe also occupied the right-half and inside right berths, skippering Albion from all three positions.

He was born in Wolverhampton in October 1935 and, after unsuccessful trials at Molineux, became a professional with Albion on his seventeenth birthday in 1952. He went on to appear in almost 380 first-team games for the Baggies. He took over the number two shirt from Stuart Williams and between Christmas 1955 and April 1964 was a permanent fixture in the side, missing only a few games (mainly due to international duty). He replaced polio victim Jeff Hall in the England side and gained all of his 23 full caps consecutively – the first against Wales in October 1957, the last versus Northern Ireland in November 1959. Four of these came in the 1958 World Cup finals in Sweden, when he partnered Tommy Banks of Bolton Wanderers and lined up behind fellow Albion team-mates Bobby Robson and Kevan Kevan. Besides his senior international honours, Howe also represented his country at Under 23 and 'B' team levels; he starred for the Football League side, the FA XI in 1956 and 1962 and toured New Zealand with the FA party in 1961.

After several disputes with Albion manager Jimmy Hagan, one being the infamous tracksuit saga, when players were made to train in shorts on bitterly cold days, Howe was transferred to Arsenal. Unfortunately, he fractured his right leg in March 1966 against Blackpool at Highbury and never played again. Howe was the Arsenal coach when they won the double in 1970/71 and in the late 1970s he coached the Gunners to three Wembley cup finals and a European Cup Winners Cup final appearance.

He was not overly successful in his period in charge of his former club West Brom, who were relegated from the First Division in 1973 after twenty-four years in the top flight. A spell as a coach with Galatasary in Turkey and a similar appointment at Leeds United preceded a return to Highbury as coach in 1977. He then became caretaker-manager of Arsenal following the departure of Terry Neill in December 1983 and signed some excellent players, although the Gunners never came close to winning any major prizes under his control. He asked to be released from his post when Terry Venables applied (albeit unsuccessfully) for the job.

Howe was coach of Wimbledon when they won the FA Cup in 1988 before reluctantly taking over team affairs at Queen's Park Rangers (although he was officially chief coach at Loftus Road). In January 1992 he replaced Terry

Left: Howe checking an attack at The Hawthorns in 1958. Right: Ready to clear his lines during a League game on a snow-covered pitch against Charlton at The Valley.

Butcher as manager of Coventry City, eventually agreeing an eighteen-month contract. Howe was joined at Highfield Road in May 1992 by joint-manager Bobby Gould, whom he had signed as a player for West Brom back in 1971. The two men worked together for barely eight weeks before Howe accepted an offer to become Ian Porterfield's assistant at Chelsea. He had been suffering with a heart problem and chose to return to London to avoid travelling up and down the country. Howe has been part of the England coaching set-up since 1977 and was also assistant to manager Ron Greenwood for five years. He is presently director of youth coaching at Highbury. Howe is regarded as one of Europe's finest coaches and players who have served with him will confirm this. When he was manager at The Hawthorns, one or two players stayed behind for extra coaching from Howe.

Lee Hughes
Striker, 1997-2001

Football League:	137+19	78
FA Cup:	6	2
League Cup:	10+3	4
Others:	2	1
Total:	155+22	85

Lee Hughes made a tremendous start to his Football League career, scoring 14 goals (all in the League) in 41 senior appearances (21 as a substitute) in his first season. He hasn't looked back since, firing in plenty more goals for the Baggies, including 32 in 1998/99, 15 the following season and more than 20 in 2000/01.

He joined Albion in May 1997 for £250,000 from Kidderminster Harriers, the then Vauxhall Conference side, and was immediately taken to by the supporters. He has pace, aggression, shooting power and heading ability, and simply loves scoring goals. Occasionally falling foul of the referee, he has served his fair share of suspensions since becoming a Baggie but he will never cease from being a totally committed, all-action footballer who will never, ever forget the day he scored a penalty against Wolves.

Born in Smethwick in May 1976, and a keen Brummie Road Ender as a youngster, Hughes was capped 4 times by England at semi-professional level whilst at Aggborough. He had trials with both Albion and Wolves before joining Kidderminster. Hughes appeared in more than 175 senior games for Albion and scored over 80 goals, a fine record.

He has a positive, all-action style and loves to run at defenders, usually coming in from a wide angle either on the right or left. He seems to prefer his right foot but can use his left to good effect as well A fine penalty taker, he has only missed once from the spot for the Baggies – in a Worthington Cup game at home to Derby County early in the 2000/01 season. During that campaign Hughes became the target of several top-line clubs, including Coventry City and Everton, but Albion boss Gary Megson declined to sell – that is until relegated Coventry City came in with a £5 million offer in August 2001. Hughes – Albion's record sale – departed, perhaps reluctantly, after scoring a goal every two games for the Baggies, saying: 'I gave the club good value for money and I did my bit for the team I loved.'

Hughes himself, deep down, is a Baggies man through and through and he would dearly love to score goals at Old Trafford, Elland Road and Highbury (and indeed in Europe) wearing a navy blue and white striped shirt.

NB – Hughes scored two hat-tricks in the space of eleven days in November 1998, both in the League against Crystal Palace and Huddersfield Town; earlier in the season he had netted three in a game against Port Vale.

Andy Hunt
Striker, 1993-98

Football League:	201+11	76
FA Cup:	7	2
League Cup:	12	4
Other:	8+1	3
Total:	228+12	85

The loan-signing by Albion boss Ossie Ardiles of striker Andy Hunt from Newcastle United in March 1993 was the key to promotion that season! The twenty-two-year-old from Grays in Essex, who had been released by Norwich City as a youngster, made a dramatic impact by scoring some crucial goals for the Baggies, including a hat-trick on his home debut against Brighton & Hove Albion and decisive ones in both the Second Division play-off semi-final and final against Swansea City and Port Vale respectively.

A tall, well-built footballer, who was quick and had good, close control and powerful shots (in both feet), Hunt did exceedingly well with Albion, who secured his transfer on a permanent basis for £100,000 soon after that Wembley success in 1993.

Linking up splendidly, firstly with Bob Taylor and then Lee Hughes and the Canadian international Paul Peschisolido, Hunt went on to net a goal every three games for the Baggies.

His best season was in 1995/96 when he struck 17 goals (14 in the League), helping Albion to pull clear of relegation over the final six weeks of the campaign.

The following season (with Hughes his main striking partner), he again contributed greatly to Albion's goal-tally and did likewise in 1997/98. This kind of form quickly led to his transfer to Charlton Athletic on the Bosman ruling in the summer of 1998.

He went on to score plenty of goals for the Addicks and helped them regain their Premiership status in 1999/2000 after losing it the year before. Unfortunately, Hunt missed practically all of the 2000/01 campaign with a viral illness. And it came as a big surprise when in June 2001 he announced that he was retiring from first-class football.

Born in June 1970, Hunt, once a trialist with Norwich City, joined Newcastle United as a full-time professional from Kettering Town in 1991. He scored 14 goals in 51 outings for the Geordies.

55

George James
Centre forward, 1920-29

Football League:	106	52
FA Cup:	10	5
Total:	118	54

A short, heavily-built inside or centre forward of the bustling type, George James once scored a goal five seconds after kick-off at the start of a First Division game at The Hawthorns. Playing for Albion against Nottingham Forest in December 1924, he netted from twenty yards past startled goalkeeper Bennett after a mazy dribble by Joe Carter. James scored four times in that 5-1 victory and went on to register an average of a goal in almost every two games during his time with the Baggies – including 30 in that 1924/25 campaign (his best return for the club).

A positive footballer, who was fearless and had a powerful right-foot shot, he teamed up superbly with Carter, Stan Davies and Tug Wilson during his Albion career before losing his place to Jimmy Cookson.

Born in Oldbury in February 1899, James joined Albion from Bilston United in January 1920.

He made his Football League debut against Bolton Wanderers at Burnden Park in November 1921 when he replaced Bobby Blood. He gained a regular place in the first team towards the end of the 1923/24 campaign (taking over the centre forward berth from Stan Davies) and thereafter he was in control, playing very well at times and scoring regularly.

However, despite his presence and firepower, Albion slithered down the First Division table and suffered relegation at the end of the 1926/27 season – just two years after finishing runners-up! As a result of this, James lost his place in the side to a new signing, Jimmy Cookson from Chesterfield. He played well enough in the reserves but could not get back into the senior side. In fact, he managed only one first team appearance in 1927/28 and eleven more in the League the following year.

He remained at The Hawthorns until May 1929 when he moved to Reading, afterwards assisting Watford before retiring in 1933 when he returned to West Bromwich to become a publican.

He died in December 1976.

Claude Jephcott
Outside right, 1911-23

Football League:	174	15
FA Cup:	15	-
Other:	1	-
Total:	190	16

Claude Jephcott was a brilliant outside right – being both fast and skilful, he was also wonderfully consistent and a player who always rose to the big occasion. Unfortunately, his career ended after breaking a leg during the local derby with Aston Villa in September 1922 when he was in sight of his 200th senior appearance for the club.

Twelve months prior to that mishap, the blond-haired Jephcott had been in excellent form when he suffered a bad injury playing against Middlesbrough at Ayresome Park. He was out of action for almost eight months and then, after regaining full fitness, he suffered another shattering blow at Villa Park.

Before the First World War, Jephcott – following his League debut against Sunderland in December 1911 – had escaped serious injury. In fact, he only missed four games in two-and-a-half years before being sidelined with a knee injury in 1914/15.

He had a fine temperament and would often tap his opponent on the back or head if he had robbed him of the ball in a 50-50 challenge. Jephcott himself was a honest professional who gave everything he had on the pitch ... and a lot more of it as well. He often helped the younger players at the club during the afternoon following the morning training session and there is no doubt that he would have made a very fine coach. His skipper Jesse Pennington stayed behind to assist on several occasions.

Born in Smethwick in October 1891, Jephcott was recruited by Albion from Brierley Hill Alliance in April 1911 after several players had been used on the right wing (without success) during the previous three years.

He immediately linked up with Harry Wright and was a key member of the Albion team that reached the FA Cup final in 1912 and won the League title in 1920 (when he scored 5 goals in 21 appearances, sharing the right-wing berth with Jack Crisp). He represented the Football League in 1913, an England XI in 1919, and guested for Birmingham, Derby County and Nottingham Forest during the First World War. After that crucial injury at Villa Park, the unlucky Jephcott announced his retirement in May 1923, aged just thirty-one.

Eleven years later he joined the board of directors at The Hawthorns and remained in office until his death in October 1950.

Willie Johnston
Outside left, 1972-79

Football League:	203+4	18
FA Cup:	24+2	6
League Cup:	15	2
Other:	12+1	2
Total:	254+7	28

With devastating pace and the ability to beat his full-back on the outside, left-winger Willie Johnston was, without doubt, a terrific footballer – but one with a fiery temper which got him into trouble with authority far too often. Nobody was faster over thirty or forty yards than Johnston, who could use both feet and centre on the run. He was a welcome acquisition in a defence-orientated game.

During his ten years at Ibrox, he was a star performer for Rangers, winning medals galore and helping them clinch their first European trophy, the 1972 Cup-Winners' Cup, when he played quite brilliantly in the final against Moscow Dynamo, netting twice in a 3-2 victory. He also won the first of his 22 full caps for Scotland whilst at Ibrox, contributing greatly in a 4-1 win over Wales at Hampden Park in November 1965. In 1971 Johnston scored a hat-trick of penalties for Rangers against St Johnstone in a League Cup-tie after coming on as a substitute – making him the first player in Scotland to achieve this feat.

West Bromwich Albion manager Don Howe signed Johnston for a club record fee of £138,000 shortly after he had served a record

sixty-seven day suspension. During his professional career, Johnston was sent-off no fewer than sixteen times with his various clubs and country, and was banished from Scotland's 1978 World Cup squad in Argentina following an allegation that he had unwittingly used a banned stimulant.

A big favourite with the fans, he played his first three full seasons with Albion in the Second Division, but then became one of player-manager Johnny Giles' greatest assets when promotion was gained in 1975/76. He missed just three League games that season, being part of a very active and positive Albion side that played forceful and precise attacking football. He retained his position on the left wing under manager Ronnie Allen, but when Ron Atkinson arrived at the club he chose to play Laurie Cunningham out wide rather than Johnston. This led to the Scottish winger moving abroad to Canada, where he joined Vancouver Whitecaps (who were managed by his former boss Johnny Giles).

One of Johnston's finest performances in an Albion shirt came in the First Division against Tottenham Hotspur at The Hawthorns in October 1976. At half time Spurs led 2-0, but after the break Johnston was quite magnificent. He turned Terry Naylor, the visiting right-back, inside out as he continually darted down the left flank and set up three goals as Albion stormed to a brilliant 4-2 victory.

Above: Willie Johnston, the joker in the mask (extreme right), prior to Albion's last home League game of the 1974/75 season v. Cardiff City. Below: Willie's first goal for Albion, in the home League Cup defeat by lowly Exeter City in October 1973.

After gaining a NASL Super Bowl championship medal with the Whitecaps he had a loan spell with Birmingham City and duly helped them win promotion to the First Division.

After that Johnston ventured back to Ibrox Park, had a second spell with the Whitecaps and later assisted Heart of Midlothian and South China in Hong Kong before taking up coaching, first at Tynecastle Park with Hearts, then East Fife, Raith Rovers and finally Falkirk. He was born in Glasgow in December 1946 and now runs a pub in Kirkcaldy.

Stan Jones

Centre-half, 1960-68

Football League:	239	2
FA Cup:	14	1
League Cup:	12	-
Europe:	2	-
Total:	267	3

Stan Jones was a big, burly, strong-tackling centre half, who gave West Bromwich Albion almost eight years of excellent service from May 1960 to March 1968. During that time he appeared in almost 270 first-team games for the Baggies.

Born at Highly, Shropshire in November 1938, he assisted Kidderminster Harriers (1954/55) and Wolves (as an amateur) before playing professionally for Walsall from May 1956 to May 1960.

He won a Fourth Division Championship medal with the Saddlers in his last season at Fellows Park before transferring to Albion (with team-mate Peter Billingham) for £7,000.

Eventually taking over from Joe Kennedy at the heart of the Albion defence, Stan became the cornerstone in the number five shirt and he never let the side down – always totally committed, he was positive in his style and a sound tackler who never shirked a challenge.

An ever-present in seasons 1961/62 and 1963/64, he missed only two League games in 1962/63, one in 1964/65 and four in 1965/66. He loved a challenge but was only ever cautioned twice and never sent off. Like most defenders, he occasionally had a lapse of concentration and conceded three own goals in one season (two in successive matches).

After twice missing out on a League Cup final place (in 1966 when he was replaced by Danny Campbell and in 1967 when Dennis Clarke took over the mantle) he finally lost his place in the side to John Talbut.

On leaving The Hawthorns, Stan returned to the Saddlers and he took his appearance tally with the Fellows Park club to an almost exactly to that he had achieved with the Baggies. As his career wound down he assisted Burton Albion, Kidderminster Harriers (again, this time as player-manager) and Hednesford Town, later coaching Coleshill Town, before becoming Walsall's trainer for seven years, from 1980 to 1987.

Stan, who assisted the Albion All Stars in more than 60 charity matches, now lives in Walsall and runs a sports-outfitters business.

John Kaye

Forward/half-back/defender, 1963-71

Football League:	281+3	45
FA Cup:	25	2
League Cup:	31	6
Europe:	10	1
Other:	11	-
Total:	358+3	54

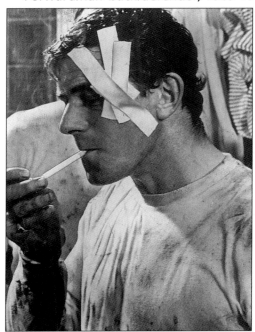

John 'Yorky' Kaye was a goalscoring inside right when he joined Albion from Scunthorpe United for a club record fee of £44,750 in May 1963 – he was signed to replace Derek Kevan. He was joined in Albion's attack by Jeff Astle a year later and between them they netted well over 100 goals before Kaye was successfully converted into a defensive left half as Albion headed for Wembley and the 1968 FA Cup final. Kaye replaced the unfortunate Eddie Colquhoun in the half-back line, where he became an excellent partner to the redoubtable John Talbut.

During his eight-year stay at The Hawthorns, Kaye made hundreds of friends and no enemies (apart from his opponents on the pitch). He was a dedicated professional who at times played straight through the pain barrier.

His terrific display in the sixth round FA Cup replay against Liverpool at Maine Road in April 1968, when he battled on bravely with his head swathed in bandages, will long be remembered by the fans who were present that evening as one of the most courageous displays ever produced by an Albion player. He also had his head heavily bandaged during the local derby against Wolves in October 1964 but, brave as he was, he still scored twice in a marvellous 5-1 victory.

Wherever he lined up – at right-back, wing-half, centre half, inside right or centre forward – 'Yorky' Kaye was totally committed ...

Playing with such dedication, endeavour, wholehearted commitment and resilience, Kaye helped Albion win the League Cup in 1966, the FA Cup in 1968 and reach the 1967 and 1970 League Cup finals, as well as the quarter-final stage of the European Cup Winners' Cup. Kaye played twice for the Football League, was voted Midland Footballer of the Year in 1966 and 1970 and played in well over 350 senior games for Albion before moving to Hull City for £28,000 in November 1971.

He was later appointed coach and then manager at Boothferry Park, was assistant manager at his former club Scunthorpe and became a key figure at Briggs Sports FC in the 1990s, having previously assisted Goole Town and Brigg Town.

Joe Kennedy

Centre-half, 1948-61

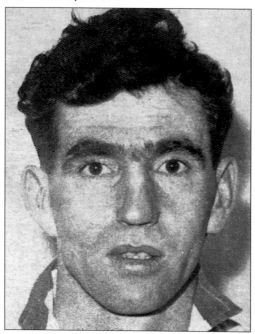

Football League:	364	3
FA Cup:	32	1
Other:	1	-
Total:	397	4

Raven-haired Joe Kennedy was a cool, commanding centre half who gave Albion excellent service for more than twelve-and-a-half years. One of the best uncapped players to represent the club, he joined the Baggies initially as an inside right. He was subsequently converted into a very useful attacking right-half and ended up as an England candidate for the centre half position, being named as reserve to Billy Wright on a number of occasions without ever receiving a call up to the national side. He did, however, skipper his country as a 'B' international, winning 3 caps at this level.

Tremendous in the air, sound and sure on the ground, Kennedy very rarely committed a foul, was hardly ever cautioned and never sent-off, and his motto was simple: when in doubt, kick it out.

He was as steady as a rock. While not the fastest of defenders, he was a fine positional player who was hardly ever given the runaround by an inside or centre forward. Rarely caught out of place, one feels that he would have been an exceptionally fine player in today's tactical game involving the twin centre half or sweeper systems.

Born in Cleator Moor near Whitehaven in November 1925, he was a teenage trialist with Brentford and Millwall before being lured to The Hawthorns from Altrincham in December 1948. He helped the team climb out of the Second Division straightaway, playing in the last eight matches of that successful season and scoring a vital goal in the 3-0 win at Leicester City which secured promotion. Unable to hold down a first-team place in the forward line, he switched to defence and, after a spell at wing-half, was nurtured to take over the number five jersey from Irish international Jack Vernon. However, he had to battle hard and long with young Jimmy Dugdale for his first team place and, in fact, Kennedy lost his position in the side halfway through the 1953/54 campaign when Albion were going great guns as they sought to capture the League and FA Cup double. Thankfully, from Kennedy's point of view, an untimely injury to Stan Rickaby allowed him back into the team in the unaccustomed right-back position and he went on to help the Baggies win at Wembley, Kennedy himself starting the move which led to the winning goal against Preston North End.

After Dugdale had moved to Villa Park in 1956, Kennedy (except in the 1958/59 campaign when he was injured) was Albion's regular centre half until Stan Jones arrived in 1960. He left The Hawthorns at the same time as Ronnie Allen, joining Chester, and, after retiring from soccer in 1966, Kennedy worked for the West Bromwich-based company Brockhouse & Son until his death in September 1986.

Derek Kevan
Centre forward, 1953-63

Football League:	262	157
FA Cup:	29	16
Total:	291	173

Known as 'The Tank', centre forward Derek Kevan was a huge fellow, standing just over six feet tall and weighing around 13 stones. He had power in every department as well as a big heart, heaps of stamina and a lust for goals.

Full of Yorkshire pluck, grit and determination, he was a tremendously competitive footballer; a rugged striker, he loved battling it out with the toughest defenders in the game. Kevan possessed great heading ability, packed a powerful shot in both feet and was always totally committed. His bustling tactics were not viewed with unalloyed approval by some critics but no one could deny he made his presence felt. He looked awkward at times, but what a goalscorer – he netted 235 times in 440 League appearances for his eight clubs.

Born in Ripon in March 1936, Kevan was manager Vic Buckingham's first signing for West Bromwich Albion, arriving at The Hawthorns as a raw teenager in 1953. He spent two years in the reserves before scoring twice on his First Division debut against Everton in August 1955. After establishing himself in the first team in 1956, he teamed up superbly with Ronnie Allen and Bobby Robson, and at times with Brian Whitehouse, in Albion's front line during the late 1950s. Kevan himself was Albion's top marksman on six occasions, scoring a total of 34 competitive goals in 1961/62. In March 1960 he became the last Albion player to score five goals in a game when Everton were defeated 6-2 at The Hawthorns. In 1957/58, Albion's forwards had a stunning season – Kevan hit 23, Allen 28 and Robson 27: a total of 78 goals for Albion out of the team's total of 112.

Kevan bid farewell to his adoring Albion fans with a hat-trick in a 6-1 home win over Ipswich Town in March 1963 … a week later the Baggies lost 7-0 to Wolves. Kevan also scored 8 goals in his 14 international appearances for England, making a scoring debut in a 2-1 win over Scotland at Wembley in April 1957. He also did well in the 1958 World Cup finals in Sweden, netting against Russia and Austria.

After scoring a goal for every 151 minutes of playing time for Albion, he moved to Chelsea (under Tommy Docherty's management). His stay at Stamford Bridge was a relatively short one, lasting barely five months, but he did help the Blues gain promotion from the Second Division. Moving on to Manchester City, he set a new post-war scoring record of 30 goals in 1963/64 when partnering Jimmy Murray in attack. During his time at Maine Road Kevan thrived on the service provided by left-winger Dave Wagstaffe, but when 'Waggy' moved to Wolverhampton Wanderers in December 1964, Kevan followed him out of Maine Road, signing for Crystal Palace at the end of that season. Thereafter 'The Tank' did his loyal duty with Peterborough United, Luton Town and Stockport County, picking up the only club medal of his entire playing career at Edgeley

Derek Kevan playing in his last international for England, an 8-0 win over Mexico at Wembley in May 1961.

Park when the Fourth Division Championship was won in 1966/67.

In 1968 he entered non-League soccer with Macclesfield Town and, after serving with Boston United, Stourbridge and Ansells FC, he finally retired in 1975, although he did play regularly in charity matches for the WBA Old Stars until 1985. Kevan was a lottery manager at The Hawthorns during the mid-1980s and he now lives in retirement with his wife, Connie, in Birmingham.

George Lee
Outside left, 1949-58

Football League:	271	59
FA Cup:	23	6
Other:	1	-
Total:	295	65

George 'Ada' Lee was born in York in June 1920. A wholehearted player, he was a dashing outside-left, fast, decisive and strong, who varied his game and style judiciously. Well-built and able to withstand the heftiest of challenges, he packed a powerful left-foot shot and scored several of his goals with low drives from the edge of the area or just outside. His pace was his biggest asset, racing onto long passes pumped down the wing – and he could cross a ball on the run with perfection.

After serving his Football League apprenticeship with York City, the raven-haired Lee enhanced his technique with Nottingham Forest before becoming an established First Division player with West Bromwich Albion. He was signed in July 1949 by manager Jack Smith for £12,000 ... after the Baggies had utilised no fewer than NINE different players in the number eleven shirt the previous season when gaining promotion from the Second Division.

Playing in an attack-minded formation with five forwards all going for goal, Lee had a moderate first season in the top flight, but in 1950/51 he came out of his shell and over the next four years some his performances were of international standard. He helped Albion win the FA Cup and finish runners-up in the First Division in 1953/54, missing only one game that season.

He had an excellent game in the Cup final against Preston North End and set up Ronnie Allen's opening goal with a precise low centre from the left.

There is no doubt he performed extremely well during his nine-year stay at The Hawthorns, which ended in June 1958 when he joined Lockheed Leamington; he later assisted Vauxhall Motors. He returned to The Hawthorns as trainer (1959-63) and then became trainer-coach with Norwich City, seeing the Canaries win the Second Division title in 1971/72.

Lee remained at Carrow Road until 1987 and lived in Norwich for the remainder of his life. He died there in April 1991 at the age of seventy.

Roddy McLeod
Inside forward, 1891-97

Football League:	149	50
FA Cup:	20	7
Other:	16	8
Total:	185	65

Roddy McLeod was a grand little player who occupied the inside right position with England international Billy Bassett as his outside partner. The chunky McLeod, who was made of Scottish granite, was a talented footballer with intricate skills.

He possessed a powerful right-foot shot, had excellent passing ability and averaged a goal every three games for Albion. He made an immediate impact at the club, helping Albion win the FA Cup in his first full season in English football (1891 *v*. Aston Villa) and he also appeared on the losing side in the final three years later, also against the Villa.

Linking up superbly with right-winger Billy Bassett, McLeod regularly took the bulk of the weight away from his international colleague as he battled hard and long in Albion's forward line. He was a real grafter, always eager and active out on the field, never wavering and often acting as the buffer when the going got tough.

He scored some fine goals – one of his best coming against Blackburn Rovers in a first round FA Cup-tie in January 1894. He also netted a beauty in another cup game against Grimsby Town two years later and scored two real gems in a League match against Wolverhampton Wanderers at Molineux in December 1893. That day the Baggies won in style by 8-0 and McLeod grabbed a hat-trick.

Born in Stirlingshire in February 1872, he played for Kilsyth and Kirkintillock schools and Partick Thistle prior to moving to Albion in January 1891.

On leaving West Bromwich he signed for Leicester Fosse (April 1897) and later assisted Brighton United, Southampton (1899/1900) and Brentford, helping the Bees win the Southern League championship in 1900/01 before ending his playing days in May 1906. McLeod later moved to London, where he worked in a brewery before becoming a mechanic. He took early retirement due to rheumatoid arthritis, a legacy from his playing days.

He died in Lambeth in December 1931.

Bobby McNeal

Left-half, 1910-22

Football League:	370	9
FA Cup:	30	-
Other:	3	1
Total:	403	10

Bobby McNeal, 5ft 6in tall and 11st in weight, was a tough-tackling wing half and a resolute and confident defender who tried to use the ball rather than simply hoofing it downfield in the hope of finding a team-mate.

Born in County Durham in January 1891, he played his early football with Hobson Wanderers before joining Albion in June 1910 as a long-term replacement for Jack Manners.

He actually made his League debut at the age of nineteen, four months later, lining up at inside-left against Leeds City. He remained in that position for the next two matches before switching into the half-back line where he remained until 1925, when niggling knee and ankle injuries started to interrupt his performances on a far too regular basis.

In spite of these problems, he was a very consistent performer and lined up in well over 400 first-class games for the Baggies, a record that places him in the club's all-time list of appearance-makers.

He helped Albion win the Second Division title in his first season with the club when he formed a splendid middle-line alongside George Baddeley and Frank Waterhouse. Twelve months later he played in the FA Cup final defeat by Barnsley when his midfield colleagues were Sid Bowser and Fred Buck, and eight years later – the first campaign after the First World War – he gained a First Division championship medal after Albion had swept all before them, amassing 60 points, scoring over 100 goals and winning 28 matches – these were all records at the time.

McNeal, who skippered Albion several times, represented the Football League on five occasions, all before 1915, and was capped twice by England – against Wales and Scotland in 1913/14.

During the hostilities he guested for Everton, Port Vale, Notts County, Middlesbrough and Fulham, starring for the Cottagers in the London Victory Cup final at Highbury. On his retirement in the summer of 1925, at the age of thirty-four, he was appointed coach at The Hawthorns, a position he held for two years.

McNeal later became a West Bromwich publican and died in the town in May 1956.

Tommy Magee
Inside forward/right-half, 1919-33

Football League:	394	15
FA Cup:	34	-
Other:	6	3
Total:	434	18

Tommy Magee, known as 'The Pocket Hercules' and 'Mighty Midget', became a West Bromwich Albion player while serving in the forces in France, signing the appropriate papers in the trenches in January 1919.

At 5ft 2in tall (and less than 11 stone in weight) he was the smallest and lightest player ever to appear for the club at senior level and it wasn't until 1991 that he lost that distinction!

Initially an inside right, full of commitment and energy, he was given his Football League debut in the opening game of the 1919/20 season against Oldham Athletic. He held his position until early February, when he was replaced by Andy Smith. He had made 24 appearances and scored 7 goals which entitled him to a League Championship medal as the Baggies took the title to make Magee's first season of competitive football one to remember.

He spent most of the following campaign in the reserves and in 1921/22 was called into the side at outside-right before taking over the right-half position from Sammy Richardson in 1922. He remained an Albion regular (injuries apart) until 1933, when he handed over the duties to Jimmy Murphy.

A great favourite with the fans, Magee became the first Albion player to win both League and FA Cup winners medals when he proudly added the latter prize to his collection when Birmingham were defeated 2-1 in the 1931 Cup Final at Wembley. Magee worked his socks off that afternoon on a sodden pitch, producing one of his finest performances in a Baggies shirt.

He twice toured Canada with the FA party, first in 1926 and then in 1931. He also gained 5 full caps for England between 1922 and 1925, lining up against Wales, Sweden, Belgium, Scotland and France. He was also an international trialist.

Born in Widnes in May 1899, Magee played rugby football locally with Appleton Hornets and the St Helens Recreational Club before joining his first soccer club, Widnes Athletic, as an amateur in 1915. He then went off to fight for his country, returning as a professional with the Albion.

He served at The Hawthorns for fifteen years, making well over 400 senior appearances up to May 1934, when he left to join Crystal Palace as player-coach.

In the summer of 1935, he became player-manager of non-League Runcorn, whom he later coached before quitting football in 1947. Magee died in his native Widnes in May 1974.

Football League:	193	7
FA Cup:	16	-
Total:	200	7

One of Albion's unsung heroes, John Albert (Jack) Manners was a very competent defender. Predominantly a left-sided player, he could perform either as a stopper centre half or left half. He had excellent passing ability, possessed a strong tackle and was a smart header of the ball, as well as being very reliable.

Born in the hot-bed of soccer in the north-east of England at Morpeth in March 1878, he played for his local YMCA team and for the town club Morpeth Harriers before joining Albion in May 1904, signed to take over the centre half position from Jim Stevenson.

He made his debut on the opening day of the 1904/05 season, in a 4-1 win at Burnley, and held his position, injuries apart, until 1910 when Bobby McNeal, also from the north-east, came along to eventually take over his duties.

In that six-year period, Manners was certainly one of the mainstays of the team. He formed part of a solid middle-line that also contained Arthur Randle and Ted Pheasant, George Baddeley and Sammy Timmins. He played in the 1907 FA Cup semi-final defeat by Everton and helped the Albion win the Second Division Championship in 1911, although only appearing in twelve games.

He started the 1911/12 season in the centre half position but missed out on an FA Cup final appearance after losing his place halfway through the campaign when Fred Buck was moved into the half-back line at his expense.

Manners remained at The Hawthorns for a further twelve months, until June 1913, when he returned home to sign for Hobson Wanderers, later becoming player-manager of

Hartlepool United in July 1919 and retiring in May 1920. Four years later he returned to the same club as team manager, a position he held for three seasons, until July 1927. His best season in charge of the 'Pool was in 1925/26, when he guided them to sixth place in the Third Division (North). The team scored plenty of goals that season and one of their finest displays was beating Walsall 9-3.

Manners died in the north-east of England in May 1946.

Len Millard

Wing-half/left-back, 1937-58

Football League:	436	7
FA Cup:	40	-
Other:	149	11
Total:	625	18

Len 'Dependable' Millard, also known as the 'Agitator', was West Bromwich Albion's regular left full-back for eight years from April 1949 until April 1957, and he captained the side for most of that time.

Five years after helping Albion to win promotion from the Second Division in 1948/49, he led the team to the runners-up spot in the First Division and also captained the Baggies to a memorable 3-2 victory over Preston North End in the FA Cup final. He was thirty-five at the time, but his vast experience helped control the threat of England international right-winger Tom Finney. He was also in the team when the Baggies reached the FA Cup semi-finals three seasons later. A steady footballer, who was never booked or sent-off, Millard was fortunate enough to avoid serious injury and he missed only 13 first-team matches during the ten immediate post-war seasons, being an ever-present twice.

A clean kicker of the ball, Millard very rarely ventured past the halfway line once he had settled down in the left-back position. In fact, he only scored three goals while wearing the number three shirt, two in the 1954/55 campaign. His first was a late equaliser in a 3-3 draw against the champions-to-be Chelsea at Stamford Bridge in October and the second was a thumping drive high into the net from thirty yards which earned Albion a 1-0 home win over Cardiff City in late December. His third effort was a sweetly struck penalty, which gained Albion a point at Old Trafford on the last day of the 1956/57 season.

Millard played in only one more first team game after that encounter against Manchester United – *v.* Leeds at Elland Road in October 1957.

Born in Coseley in March 1919, Millard played for several local teams before signing as a junior at The Hawthorns in May 1937 (from Sunbeam FC). He made 150 appearances for Albion during the Second World War, when he occupied several positions, including those of wing-half and centre forward (he scored two hat-tricks in 1942). But it was as a steady, reliable left-back where he performed with so much consistency during the 1950s after taking over that position from England international Harry Kinsell. He always played well against Stanley Matthews and Finney, and was very rarely 'roasted' by his opposing winger.

Twenty-one years after joining the club, Millard left the Albion to take over as manager of Stafford Rangers, his place in the side going to Welshman Stuart Williams, who earlier had been his partner at right-back until Don Howe came along in 1955. After being troubled for some time, Len had to have a leg amputated in 1989. He died in his home town of Coseley in March 1997, aged seventy-eight.

Fred Morris

Inside forward/centre forward, 1911-24

Football League:	263	112
FA Cup:	20	4
Other:	4	2
Total:	287	118

Fred Morris was a strongly built and courageous inside or centre forward who possessed rapid acceleration, a powerful right-foot shot, neat ball control and exceptional positional sense. He was a prolific goalscorer and in 1919/20, when Albion won the First Division, he netted 37 League goals, five of them coming in one match against Notts County. This tally was a club record at the time and remained so until 1927/28, when it was bettered by Jimmy Cookson.

Born in Tipton in August 1893, the ginger-haired Morris moved to The Hawthorns from Redditch in May 1911 and made his senior debut in April 1912, scoring in the 1-0 home win over Sunderland – the first of his 118 goals for the Baggies (in less than 300 appearances). He later became the first Albion player to top the century mark in goalscoring, doing so in 1922.

Morris began to establish himself in the League side during the course of the 1912/13 season, when he accompanied Bob Pailor and Sid Bowser in Albion's attack, and the following campaign he had Alf 'Snobby' Bentley and Albert Lewis alongside him. Then, with the First World War approaching, he was paired with several other front men before playing as a guest for Watford and Fulham during the hostilities. He scored numerous goals for those two clubs, including a double hat-trick for Watford against Portsmouth in February 1917.

Peace returned, and in the 1919/20 season he finally settled down at inside left (his favourite position), as part of a quite formidable forward line that comprised Claude Jephcott, Tommy Magee, Andy Smith, himself and Howard Gregory. The left-wing partnership of Morris and Gregory was regarded as one of the finest in the land and they remained in unison until 1923.

Over a period of four years (1919-23), Morris scored 80 League and cup goals, while the other forwards around him netted barely 100 goals between them! He had the knack of hitting the target practically every time he struck the ball. The 'keeper saved a lot of his goal-bound efforts, the woodwork and other defenders prevented a few more finding their way into the net, but there is no doubt that Morris was a wonderfully consistent marksman and certainly one of the finest ever to wear an Albion shirt.

A junior international in 1911, Morris gained 2 full caps for England, starring against Scotland at Sheffield in April 1920 (when he scored in a thrilling 5-4 victory) and versus Ireland at The Hawthorns six months later. He also represented the Football League and the FA.

In August 1924, after thirteen years with Albion, Morris was transferred to Coventry City. Twelve months later he entered non-League football with Oakengates Town and retired in 1930. He died in Great Bridge in July 1962.

Paddy Mulligan
Right-back, 1975-79

Football League:	109	1
FA Cup:	11	-
League Cup:	7	-
Other:	5	1
Total:	132	2

An accomplished right-back with excellent positional sense and an expert at the overlap, Paddy Mulligan was never 'taken to the cleaners' by his opposing winger. A thoughtful defender, cool under pressure, and with a lot of ability and pace, his move to Chelsea from Shamrock Rovers set up a record fee for any Republic of Ireland player up to that time.

Although rarely certain of a permanent place in the first team at Stamford Bridge, it was a disappointment to all the Chelsea supporters when he left to join Crystal Palace in 1972, having made less than 80 senior appearances for the Blues. At Selhurst Park he was never guaranteed a regular place in the side, and jumped at the chance of teaming up with the ex-Leeds United and Manchester United midfielder Johnny Giles at The Hawthorns.

Mulligan helped the Baggies gain promotion to the First Division at the end of that season, in 33 matches. He missed only two games the following season and six in 1977/78. During the latter campaign, four days after suffering FA Cup semi-final defeat against Ipswich Town at Highbury, he scored his only goal during his time at The Hawthorns – a stunning twenty-yard strike

against Newcastle United in a 2-0 victory.

Giles had left Albion in May 1977 to become player-manager of Shamrock Rovers and when Ron Atkinson, the Baggies manager, signed right-back Brendon Batson from Arsenal, Mulligan became surplus to requirements at The Hawthorns and immediately rejoined his former club and so was reunited with Giles back in Ireland.

In 1980, Mulligan was appointed assistant manager of the Greek club Panathiniakos. He returned to Ireland to take charge of Galway Rovers in August 1982 before retiring to begin an accountancy and insurance business the following year.

Born in Dublin in March 1945, Mulligan was capped by the Republic of Ireland as a fifteen-year-old schoolboy and played initially for Stella Maris (Dublin), Home Farm and the Bohemians before joining Shamrock Rovers in 1964. He also starred in the NASL with Boston Beacons. He represented the League of Ireland at the age of twenty and gained the first of his 51 full caps in 1969 against Czechoslovakia as a Shamrock Rovers player.

He won four FAI Cup winners medals with Rovers (in 1965, 1966, 1967 and 1969) and was a member of Chelsea's League Cup final side of 1972 – who were beaten 2-1 by Stoke City at Wembley. Mulligan also came on as a substitute for the London club in the European Cup-winners' Cup final against Real Madrid in Athens.

Jimmy Murphy
Wing-half, 1928-39

Football League:	204	-
FA Cup:	19	-
Total:	223	-

Nicknamed 'Spud' and 'Twinkletoes', Jimmy Murphy was a vigorous attacking wing-half, who was both strong in the tackle and a glutton for hard work, hardly stopping for a breath during the course of a game. He came to The Hawthorns at a time when the club was endeavouring to build up its senior squad soon after being relegated to the Second Division. An inside or outside left at the time, he had to wait until March 1930 before making his League debut against Blackpool (away) when he stepped in to partner Tommy Glidden on the right wing.

Thereafter, he was groomed into an international-class wing-half who went on to represent Wales in 15 internationals, winning his first full cap in November 1932 against England when skipper Fred Keenor was 'rested'. Murphy remained a regular on the international scene during the 1930s, and also became a permanent fixture in the Albion side, having claimed a place in the first team during the second-half of the 1931/32 season when he took over from Jimmy Edwards (initially) and then Tommy Magee. He went on to appear in over 220 competitive games for the Baggies, collecting a runners-up medal after Sheffield Wednesday had beat Albion 4-2 in the 1935 FA Cup final at Wembley.

Born in Ton Pentre, Glamorgan in October 1910, the son of Irish parents, Murphy played the organ at school and was capped by Wales as a schoolboy level before becoming an errand boy in 1924. He played for various junior football teams near to his home town and eventually joined Albion from Mid-Rhondda United in February 1928.

In March 1939 he left The Hawthorns to sign for Swindon Town, but when the Second World War broke out he assisted Commercial Motors at the outset and then served in the Eighth Army in Bari, Italy. Whilst out there he came into contact with Matt Busby and in 1945 Murphy was invited to become his coach at Old Trafford. Ten years later he was appointed assistant manager and in October 1956 Murphy was handed the job of managing Wales whilst still employed by United. Regarded as an exceptionally fine coach and great motivator, he acted as caretaker manager at Old Trafford when Busby was recovering in hospital after the 1958 Munich air disaster – Murphy was not on board the chartered aeroplane that crashed as he was in Cardiff, managing the Welsh national team in a World Cup qualifier against Israel and his place on the flight was taken by Bert Whalley, who sadly lost his life. Later that year Murphy guided Wales in their only appearance in the World Cup finals in Sweden. The pressure of trying to concentrate on two jobs became too much for him, however, and in 1964 Murphy gave up the Welsh post and concentrated on his duties as assistant boss with United.

In 1971 he became scout at the club and was still deeply involved with the Reds when he died in Manchester in November 1989.

Stuart Naylor

Goalkeeper, 1986-97

Football League:	354+1	-
FA Cup:	13	-
League Cup:	22	-
Other:	20	-
Total:	409+1	-

Goalkeeper Stuart Naylor was Ron Saunders' first signing for Albion when he took over as manager at The Hawthorns in February 1986. Secured from Lincoln City for £110,000, he had already made over 130 senior appearances while with the Imps as well as playing on loan for Crewe Alexandra and Peterborough United. He was an experienced campaigner and went straight into Albion's First XI (in place of Tony Godden) for the away game against Manchester United, where he was beaten three times as Jesper Olsen scored a hat-trick (two of them penalties).

Naylor missed the next game – a 5-0 defeat at Spurs – but then held on to the number one position (apart from when he suffered from a niggling knee injury) until halfway through the 1990/91 campaign, when he was temporarily replaced by Mel Rees. He came back soon afterwards and held firm until Tony Lange arrived on the scene in March 1993 – depriving Naylor of a Wembley appearance that season as Albion won promotion via the Second Division play-off final.

Naylor, though, was a dedicated and loyal clubman and he fought his way back into the side for the second part of the 1993/94 season. He performed consistently well over the next eighteen months or so before losing his place first to the veteran Nigel Spink and then to Paul Crichton.

Born in Leeds in December 1962 and a junior with Leeds City Amateurs and Yorkshire Amateurs, Naylor also had trials at Elland Road before joining Lincoln City as a professional in June 1980.

He was a commanding figure between the posts. Standing 6ft 4ins tall and weighing well over 12 stones, he was agile, a fine shot-stopper and commanded his area with authority. Capped by England at youth and 'B' team levels, he went on to appear in more than 400 first-class games (including 355 in the League, which is a record for a goalkeeper with Albion) before leaving the club in August 1996 after a well-deserved testimonial.

Naylor later assisted Exeter City and Rushden & Diamonds. His father and his uncle, Tommy, had both played for Oldham Athletic after the Second World War.

It is interesting to note that, in October 1982, Naylor was used as an emergency centre forward by Lincoln City in a League game against Newport County.

Football League:	131	58
FA Cup:	14	6
Total:	145	64

For four years, between 1953 and 1957, inside left Johnny Nicholls was regarded as one of the finest goal-poachers in the First Division. Teaming up with centre forward Ronnie Allen in the exciting West Bromwich Albion side under manager Vic Buckingham, the forward, who had trials at Molineux as a youngster, averaged a goal in every two-and-a-half games, most of them being laid on by Allen.

Nicholls, born in Wolverhampton in April 1931, was nicknamed the 'Poacher' and he had the knack of being in the right place at the right time to snap up the half-chance. Despite this talent, he grafted hard for his goals and also scored some real beauties without any assistance on the odd occasion. He wasn't a great footballer – as he freely admitted himself – but there was nobody better than 'Johnny on the Spot' when it came to finding the net.

Nicholls was given his debut as a late replacement for Allen in a cup-tie at Blackburn, and the following season hardly figured in first-team action, but in 1953/54 he hit the headlines with some sparkling performances as the Baggies went for the double. They finally had to settle for the runners-up spot in the First Division but made amends by winning the FA Cup, with hot-shot Nicholls ending up as the team's top League marksman with 28 goals. He also scored on his England debut against Scotland at Hampden Park in front of 140,000 fans, when he and his Albion colleague Ronnie Allen helped their country to a 4-2 win.

The following season Nicholls found it a lot harder to breach the opposing defence. He still netted a dozen League goals but now the opposing managers and coaches had found out ways of nullifying the darting and hitherto unnoticed runs of Nicholls.

After the arrival of Bobby Robson (from Fulham) and the emergence of a young Derek Kevan, Nicholls' first team place came under threat. He had 24 outings in 1955/56 and 17 the following year before his time ran out.

Nicholls, who netted some 200 goals for various Albion teams, wound down his senior career with a rather unhappy spell at Cardiff City and two years at Exeter City.

He then assisted Worcester City and Wellington Town and, on retiring from football, chose to live and work in Wolverhampton.

He died of a heart attack as he drove home from the Albion *v.* Middlesbrough League game in April 1995.

Dan Nurse

Right-half, 1901-05

Football League:	85	4
FA Cup:	3	-
Total:	88	4

Dan Nurse was a powerful right-half who was instrumental in helping Albion win the Second Division Championship at the first attempt in 1901/02. Not always at ease when faced with a clever ball-player, he was nevertheless an efficient, strong-tackling, determined footballer who gave nothing less than his absolute best. He loved going forward to assist his front men and was back in defence when the opposition attacked.

Born in Tipton in June 1873, Nurse played for Coseley FC before joining Wolverhampton Wanderers in the summer of 1894. He spent seven years at Molineux, mainly as a reserve, before moving to The Hawthorns, where he skippered Albion in three of his four full seasons with the club. He made almost 90 senior appearances prior to announcing his retirement with a knee injury in May 1905 – fifteen months after first complaining about the problem.

Nurse quite often committed fouls in dangerous positions and, indeed, during the first half of the 1902/03 season opposing teams scored four times from free-kicks awarded against Nurse. He also conceded two penalties and gave away an own goal. But this apart, he was a quality player and perhaps it was a pity that Albion did not capture him earlier.

A player who led by example, Nurse took over the right-half berth from Tom Perry and when he was initially injured – in December 1903 – his position was filled by Arthur Randle.

Nurse represented the Football League in 1902/03 and was perhaps unlucky not to have gained full international honours, especially during his first full season with Albion.

Five years later, in August 1910, Nurse joined the Albion board of directors and remained in office until May 1927. Just prior to his appointment as a director, he had been part of a consortium that guaranteed the players' summer wages when another financial crisis loomed. He was elected a life member of the club in 1920 in recognition of his sterling efforts in keeping the club in existence. Nurse died in April 1959.

NB – Dan's brother, Lou, was an Albion director for twenty-six years (1922-48). He had acted as scout for the club before joining the board. He had a particular interest in the reserve team and during a fifteen-year period he missed only two Central League matches. He was elected Albion chairman in 1937 and was also an FA Councillor.

John Osborne

Goalkeeper, 1967-78

Football League:	250	-
FA Cup:	24	-
League Cup:	16	-
Europe:	8	-
Other:	14	-
Total:	312	-

An excellent goalkeeper, and certainly one of the finest to appear for West Bromwich Albion, John Osborne, 'Ossie' to his fans, was worth every penny of the £10,000 manager Jimmy Hagan paid Chesterfield for his services in January 1967. He appeared in more than 300 competitive matches during his eleven years at The Hawthorns, which were divided into two spells.

Alert and intelligent – both as a footballer and in quizzes – Osborne was courageous and commanding. He suffered several hand injuries during his career, which resulted in a strip of plastic being inserted into one of his fingers, hence his title the 'bionic goalkeeper'. He never let that bother him, and continued to be brave and daring, often throwing himself at the feet of onrushing forwards. In a vital sixth round FA Cup-tie at Chelsea in March 1969, he went diving in amongst flying feet to retrieve the ball as Albion clung on to a 2-1 lead. He was kicked on the head, on the arm, the shoulder and finger but, after a quick sponge-down, he put his thumbs up and carried on with the game.

Born in Barlborough, Derbyshire in December 1940, Osborne won England schoolboy honours as a wing-half before being converted into a goalkeeper at Chesterfield, a club which has produced many good custodians

over the years. During his first five years at The Hawthorns he contested the number one spot with Dick Sheppard, Jim Cumbes, Peter Latchford and Graham Smith. Later he helped Albion win the FA Cup in 1968, reach the 1970 League Cup final and play in Europe.

In 1973, 'Ossie' quit Albion to run a sports business but returned to The Hawthorns after six months. He had a loan spell with Walsall before regaining his first-team place with Albion in 1975 under manager Johnny Giles. He was in peak form when the Baggies won promotion in 1976, keeping 20 clean sheets and conceding only 33 goals – a club record.

He left The Hawthorns in 1978 to join Shamrock Rovers (managed by his former boss Giles) and thereafter acted as goalkeeping cover with several English clubs. In 1983/84 he managed non-League Corinthians FC, working also for the Sandwell Mail before becoming commercial manager of Worcestershire County Cricket Club, a position held for five years.

It was reported that he had cancer in April 1998 and, sadly, he died in December of the following year.

Gary Owen
Midfield, 1979-86

Football League:	185+2	21
FA Cup:	12+2	3
League Cup:	24	2
Europe:	4	-
Total:	225+4	26

The round-shouldered Gary Owen was an excellent midfield player who amassed a fine record of almost 230 senior appearances for the Baggies. A Lancastrian, born in St Helens in July 1958, Owen played over 120 times for Manchester City before joining Albion in May 1979 for £465,000 – two months before his Maine Road team-mate Peter Barnes arrived at The Hawthorns.

A fine ball-player with vision and commitment, Owen took over Len Cantello's position in Albion's midfield and, with Barnes on his left, he formed an excellent partnership in the 'engine room' with Bryan Robson and, later, Remi Moses. Another former Manchester City star, Steve MacKenzie, then joined the ranks and Owen again showed his worth with some excellent performances. He missed only 24 League games during his first four and a half seasons at the club, helping Albion reach both the FA Cup and League Cup semi-finals in 1982 and compete in Europe.

Unfortunately, Owen was struck down by a series of long-term injuries, including a fractured shin, gashed calf (which required a skin graft), twisted knee, badly strained thigh and several ankle complaints. However, despite missing the second half of the 1983/84 campaign, the first half of 1984/85 and most of 1985/86, he battled on as best he could, unfortunately to no avail.

He was released in the summer of 1986, after Ron Saunders had taken over as manager, and went abroad to sign for Panionios of Greece on a two-year contract. In August 1987 he returned to England to sign for Sheffield Wednesday before ending his career in Cyprus with Apoel Nicosia.

He was a jinking sort of player who loved to hold onto the ball, occasionally to the detriment of his colleagues! He packed a strong right-foot shot (when he chose to deliver) and was pretty effective from dead-ball situations, especially when he taking an in-swinging corner from the right. Composed and confident, Owen perhaps under-achieved at times, but overall he was a class player.

Capped by England at youth team level, Owen went on to appear in a record 22 Under 21 internationals for his country and he represented the Football League. He is now working for a Manchester radio station and is also deeply involved in the antique business.

Football League:	79	40
FA Cup:	13	7
Total:	92	47

Centre forward Bob Pailor was a born goalscorer; a strong, well-built footballer, his weight, allied to pace and ability, made him one of the most feared strikers in the country once he had settled in at The Hawthorns.

He averaged one goal in every two games for Albion and helped them win the Second Division Championship in 1910/11, scoring some vitally important goals, and reach the FA Cup final the following season, when his brilliant strike in the semi-final against Blackburn took the Baggies through to meet Barnsley.

Born in Stockton-on-Tees in July 1887, Pailor played for West Hartlepool before transferring to The Hawthorns in October 1908. Albion had been struggling to fill the centre forward berth following the departure of Fred Shinton and they saw Pailor as just the man for the job.

He was nurtured in the second team, slowly being introduced into League action and once he had established himself at the start of the 1910/11 campaign he never looked back, netting a total of 12 goals that season and following up with 13 in 1911/12 and 16 the following term.

During that 1911/12 campaign Pailor, with Harry Wright and Sid Bowser either side of him for most of the time, was outstanding. He netted some cracking goals including a wonderful hat-trick in a 3-1 home win over Newcastle United in February. He also cracked in a beauty when Albion beat Everton 1-0 and did likewise in the third round FA Cup win in front of a record crowd at Sunderland. The great Charlie Buchan who

played for the home side in this game, said afterwards: 'Pailor's goal was magnificent – I just wish I can score some like that.'

Pailor had his best scoring season for Albion in 1912/13 when he notched 16 goals in the First Division including two more hat-tricks, away at Villa Park and Blackburn. Albion won both matches 4-2.

However, injuries then started to interrupt his progress and in July 1914, after Alf Bentley had taken over his position as leader of the attack, he moved back up north to sign for Newcastle United. Unfortunately, a serious kidney complaint forced him into early retirement some ten months later, at the age of just twenty-eight. After the First World War, Pailor became a very successful bookmaker.

He also ran a pub in Hartlepool before he started to go blind in the late 1950s. Pailor died in Hartlepool in January 1976.

Harold Pearson
Goalkeeper, 1925-37

Football League:	281	-
FA Cup:	21	-
Other:	1	-
Total:	303	-

For a man who stood 6ft 2in tall and weighed almost 14 stones, Harold Pearson made goalkeeping look easy. Equally adept at dealing with high or low crosses, he had a tremendous reach, a safe pair of hands (especially under pressure), and could also throw a ball up to 50 yards – usually finding his target. He was, however, occasionally hesitant on his line, sometimes lost concentration at crucial times and his kicking was somewhat erratic. Nevertheless, he gave Albion excellent service and appeared in more than 300 first-class games, helping the team win the double in 1930/31 and reach the Cup Final again in 1935. In that 1935 FA Cup final defeat by Sheffield Wednesday, Pearson blamed himself for two of Wednesday's goals, including a crucial one late on when the scores were level at 2-2. He should have gone and collected the ball but he hesitated and as a result Ellis Rimmer capitalised to put the Owls in the driving seat. The Yorkshire club scored again soon afterwards and as a result Pearson angrily turned round and smashed the ball into the net after it had rebounded.

Pearson could be caring at times, and in front of almost 70,000 fans at Old Trafford for the 1931 FA Cup semi-final against Everton, he assisted stewards, police and first aid officials by carrying injured spectators to safety. He was also capped by England against Scotland at Wembley in 1932, having represented his country in a junior international during 1927.

Born in Tamworth in May 1908, the son of Hubert Pearson, Albion's number one from 1906 to 1923, and related to Harry Hibbs, the Birmingham and England 'keeper, Pearson junior played for several local teams before joining Albion from Tamworth Castle in April 1925 (whilst his father was still at the club).

He made his senior debut in December 1927 and established himself in the first team in 1929 in place of George Ashmore. He then slipped back into the reserves before regaining his League place in March 1930. He retained it until 1936, when he came under pressure from Billy Light and then Jimmy Adams.

Pearson, nicknamed 'Algy', was an unassuming chap, who was great in the dressing room and always willing to pass on his experience to the younger players. He left Albion for Millwall in August 1937 and in his first season at The Den helped the Lions win the Third Division (South) Championship. He retired in 1940 (having also guested for West Ham United) and later returned as coach at The Hawthorns from 1948 to 1952. For many years he worked at the West Bromwich firm of Accles & Pollock and died in West Bromwich in November 1994.

Football League:	341	2
FA Cup:	29	-
Other:	7	-
Total:	377	2

A broad-shouldered goalkeeper, who was both sound and dependable as well as daring and confident in his own ability, Bert Pearson held the club record for most League appearances by a 'keeper for seventy years (it was finally beaten by Stuart Naylor in 1996). Born in Kettlebrook, near Tamworth in May 1886, Pearson was recruited by Albion from Tamworth Athletic in February 1906.

He bided his time in the reserves before claiming a regular spot in the first-team during the second half of the 1909/10 League season, after challenging Jim Stringer for quite some time. He was in splendid form when Albion won the Second Division title the following season and played very well in 1911/12 when the Baggies reached the FA Cup final, only to lose to Barnsley in a replay. During the First World War, Pearson guested for Derby County, Birmingham and Scottish club Morton and was still in charge of the number one position at The Hawthorns when competitive football resumed in 1919.

He conceded on average a goal a game in his 39 outings when Albion won their only League Championship (to date) in 1919/20. Playing behind a resolute duo of full-backs, Joe Smith and Jesse Pennington, and a half-back trio of Sammy Richardson, Sid Bowser and Bobby McNeal, Pearson was rated one of the best 'keepers in the country.

The following season, with Devon-born George Ashmore pushing hard for a first-team place, Pearson played better than he had ever done, but a leg injury allowed Ashmore the chance to show his worth. He did well, but a resolute and determined Pearson returned to the action in November 1921 and remained the first choice 'keeper until the end of the 1922/23 campaign.

He gained a junior international cap in 1907 and was then chosen to make his senior debut for England v. France in 1923 but withdrew through injury and never got another chance. He did, however, play twice for the Football League XI (in 1914 and 1922). Pearson even had the confidence to score two penalties for Albion in League games against Bury and Middlesbrough, both at The Hawthorns in 1911/12.

Pearson retired as a player in 1926, having coached the youngsters for a year, during which time he handed on some tips to his son Harold, who was soon to become Albion's number one goalkeeper.

Bert Pearson died in Tamworth in October 1955.

Tom Pearson

Inside left, 1886-94

Football League:	138	72
FA Cup:	26	12
Other:	7	4
Total:	171	88

Tom Pearson was Albion's first marksman of real quality. An all-action, aggressive inside forward who was a fine sharp-shooter, he was as good as anyone in the country during the early years of League football. In fact, he top-scored for Albion in each of the first five League seasons, between 1888 and 1893, and one feels that if injury had not intervened when it did in the following campaign he would have scored many more goals for the club.

During those five years Pearson was outstanding. He drew up a wonderful understanding with his wingers – and they included Billy Bassett and George Woodhall on the right and Joe Wilson, John Burns and Jasper Geddes on the left. He also worked efficiently with his inside forwards, especially Jem Bayliss. Bayliss was the perfect foil for Pearson, being more composed and clever while Pearson was the more robust and penetrative of the two.

His best scoring season (at senior level) was 1889/90, when he claimed 17 goals in 22 League games, including four against Bolton Wanderers and a hat-trick against Notts County.

Born in West Bromwich in April 1866, he played for Oak Villa and West Bromwich Sandwell before joining Albion at the age of twenty. He quickly established himself in the first team and with an abundance of endurance and fire power, coupled with a good eye and the ability to find space, he banged in plenty of goals.

Pearson played for Albion in three FA Cup finals, in 1887, 1888 and 1892, collecting a winners' medal in the last two when his left-wing partners were Joe Wilson and Jasper Geddes.

Taking into account the number of goals he scored in friendly and local cup competitions, Pearson's overall tally during his eight years with Albion was probably in excess of 150.

It was a sad day for everyone associated with the club when he was told he had to quit the game on medical advice at the end of the 1893/94 season, a knee injury being the problem. In fact, Pearson was crippled by the time he was thirty and confined to a wheelchair for many years prior to his death in West Bromwich in July 1918.

Jesse Pennington
Full-back, 1903-22

Football League:	455	-
FA Cup:	39	-
Other:	2	-
Total:	496	-

Jesse Pennington was a magnificent full-back. A defender of the highest quality, he was wonderfully consistent, scrupulously fair, quick in recovery and well-balanced; he also possessed a clean kick and a splendid sense of sportsmanship. Pennington gave West Bromwich Albion Football Club nineteen years of excellent service, either side of the First World War, yet he may never have joined the Baggies if rivals Aston Villa had been more considerate. Pennington was an amateur trialist at Villa Park in 1902 but was turned away as being 'unsuitable' and immediately rejoined his former club Dudley Town, from where he switched to The Hawthorns in March 1903.

He made rapid progress after his League debut against Liverpool in September 1903 and was only dropped once, in September 1904, when replaced for one game by Welshman Llewellyn Davies. He retained his position at full-back (injuries and international call-ups excepted) right up until April 1922, having drawn up a terrific partnership with Joe Smith. When Pennington played his last competitive match for Albion (his 455th in the League, coincidentally against Liverpool), it brought his total number of senior appearances to 496 – a club record that was to stand for forty-four years until Tony Brown bettered in 1976.

Born in West Bromwich in August 1883, Pennington also assisted Langley Villa and Langley St Michael's before embarking on his splendid career with Albion. He became captain of the side and led the team to the Second Division title in 1910/11, the FA Cup final twelve months later, League Championship glory in 1919/20 and the FA Charity Shield success soon afterwards.

He was capped 25 times by England between 1907 and 1920, skippering his country twice at the age of thirty-six. He played alongside Blackburn's Bob Crompton in 23 of his internationals and he also had 9 outings for the Football League, participated in 5 international trials and had 5 games for an England XI.

Throughout his career Pennington never scored a goal and rarely, if ever, did he commit a serious foul. Albion fans wanted him to do just that in the 1912 Cup Final replay, but he declined to bring down Barnsley's Harry Tufnell, who subsequently sped away to score the winning goal in the last minute of extra-time.

From the day Pennington made his senior debut until his final outing in 1922 (nineteen years at The Hawthorns) Albion fulfilled a total of 627 competitive games (League, FA Cup and Charity Shield). Pennington was absent from 131 of them, mainly due to injury

Jesse Pennington with his pet dog outside his Hartlebury home in 1969.

and international calls, but he also missed a few in 1910 when he was in dispute with the club and signed for Kidderminster Harriers! Luckily, matters were quickly sorted out for the best, and Pennington returned to The Hawthorns. He went on playing for the Baggies for another twelve years.

In November 1913, Pennington was approached by a man who offered him money to 'fix' the result of a home League game against Everton. The Albion skipper quickly advised the club secretary who, in turn, informed the police. The culprit was duly arrested and later sentenced to jail at Stafford Crown Court.

After retiring, Pennington coached at The Hawthorns for a year. He then held similar positions with Kidderminster and at Malvern College and later scouted for Wolves and Albion (between 1950 and 1960), before moving to Hartlebury, near Stourport, where he lived until his death in a Kidderminster hospital in September 1970.

In 1969, 'Peerless' Pennington was made a life member of the club – a fitting tribute to a wonderful servant and fabulous player.

Football League:	171	12
FA Cup:	39	3
Other:	9	1
Total:	219	16

Charlie Perry was a splendid footballer who was upright, strongly built, a powerful tackler and cool under pressure. He was a defender who took control of a situation and, as the team captain, marshalled his troops accordingly. A totally committed player, Perry was the backbone of Albion's defence for more than a decade, hardly ever committing a foul tackle; he was never cautioned and was as reliable as anyone in the game, making well over 200 senior appearances for the club. Born in West Bromwich in January 1866, he attended and played for Christ Church School in the town and played for the local Strollers team before joining Albion in March 1884, turning professional a year later. Having made his first team debut for Albion against Stoke Free Wanderers in a Staffordshire Cup-tie on 30 January 1886, he was given his outing in the FA Cup three months later when Albion were defeated in the final by Blackburn Rovers.

Perry played in Albion's first-ever League game, v. Stoke (away), in September 1888. A centre half with poise and elegance, he won 3 England caps – v. Ireland in March 1890 and March 1891 and v. Wales in March 1893, being on the winning side each time, with results of 9-1, 6-1 and 6-0 respectively. He also had two outings with the Football League side and appeared in four international trials.

Perry competed in the 1887, 1888 and 1892 FA Cup finals, collecting a winners' medal in the latter two versus Preston North End and Aston Villa, when he was

outstanding in both games. Unfortunately he missed the 1895 Cup Final through injury, which eventually led to his retirement in 1896. At that point he was appointed a director of the club and remained on the board until 1902. Perry later became a West Bromwich businessman and he died in the town in July 1927.

The Perry family – well-known throughout the Black Country – was strongly associated with West Bromwich Albion Football Club for many years. Besides Charlie, there were his brothers Tom (see page 86) and Walter, who had two spells in the first team between 1886 and 1895. Between them the three Perrys made in excess of 400 first-team appearances for the club.

Four other members of the family were later engaged by Albion. Arthur, an England junior international, was a full-back in the 1920s and regularly played in the League side, while William, Edward and Eric all competed at reserve and intermediate levels during their brief stays at The Hawthorns. Eric was also a very capable cricketer with West Bromwich Dartmouth.

Tom Perry

Half-back, 1890-1901

Football League:	248	14
FA Cup:	29	-
Other:	14	1
Total:	291	15

Born in West Bromwich in August 1871, Tom Perry, like his brother Charlie, was a stalwart performer for Albion, and amassed a fine record of almost 300 first-class appearances during his eleven-year stay with the club.

A pupil at Christ Church School in West Bromwich, he played for Christ Church FC, West Bromwich Baptists and Stourbridge before joining Albion in July 1890. He made his senior debut two months later, in an unaccustomed outside left position, and played a handful of matches at inside right before becoming a very competitive and aggressive right-half.

He gained a regular place in the first team in 1892/93, playing in the same middle-line as his elder brother Charlie, and he continued to be a dominant performer up until Albion suffered relegation at the end of the first season at The Hawthorns, 1900/01.

During the first few years of that eight-year association with the club, Tom Perry played alongside his kid brother Charlie in more than fifty first-team games for Albion. They were excellent together at the heart of the defence, complimenting each other in many different ways. Tom was perhaps the more aggressive of the two, and the more adventurous. He enjoyed driving forward into enemy territory while his brother held the fort at the back. He often went up for set pieces and occasionally moved into the forward-line if one of the regular front men was injured.

Capped once by England against Wales at Wrexham in March 1898, Perry played 3 times for the Football League XI in the mid-1890s and also starred in a representative game for a Division One Select XI *v.* Aston Villa in 1894. He collected a runners-up medal when Albion lost 1-0 to the Villa in the 1895 FA Cup final and it was to that rival club that he moved in the summer of 1901.

He remained there for only a short time before retiring in January 1903. Perry later worked in West Bromwich, dying in the town in July 1927, two weeks after his brother Charlie; another of the brothers, Walter, died only a year later.

Football League:	140	20
FA Cup:	12	2
Total:	152	22

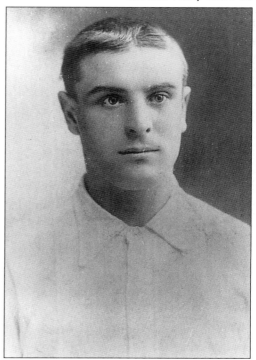

Ted 'Cock' Pheasant packed a great deal into his thirty-three years. Born in the back streets of Wednesbury in February 1877, he was initially a bustling inside or centre forward with Wednesbury Excelsior and Wednesbury Old Athletic before joining Wolves as an eighteen-year-old in the summer of 1895. In 1898/99 he was converted into a centre half and went on to make over 160 appearances for Wolves before transferring to Albion in November 1904.

A fearsome character, he would shave his head and roll up his sleeves and push his socks down to his ankles to appear as fearsome as possible to opposing forwards. Physically dominating anyway, standing 6ft 2in tall and weighing 15 stone, Pheasant was also a fierce striker of a dead ball and used to take many of the free-kicks and penalties, hitting them with tremendous power. It was said he was one of the highest paid players of his day, earning £3 10s per week during a season and £3 in the summer.

On one occasion he was selected to represent the Football League, but declined the offer, preferring to play in a League game instead – such was his dedication to club football. He took over the centre half slot from Jack Bowden at The Hawthorns and went on to make over 150 appearances for the Baggies, scoring 22 goals.

He was part of a splendid middle line that also included Arthur Randle and Jack Manners in the wing-half berths. Pheasant skippered Albion several times and was an inspiration to the rest of the team. He was often involved in the rough stuff. Surprisingly, he was rarely spoken to by the referee, certainly never sent-off, and was regarded in some quarters as one of the gentle giants in the game!

After suffering a few injury problems, and with Frank Waterhouse ready to step up from the reserves, Pheasant left Albion in July 1910, signing for Leicester Fosse, but sadly he was never able to play for the Foxes. Two weeks after leaving The Hawthorns he was admitted to a Birmingham hospital with peritonitis and he died on 17 July.

Playing for Wolves against Newcastle United at Molineux in March 1902, he scored a hat-trick from the centre half position, one of his goals – a free-kick – speeding into the net from fully thirty-five yards. It was another ninety-three years before another Wolves centre half repeated that feat.

Joe Reader

Goalkeeper, 1885-1901

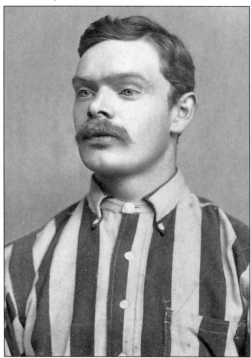

Football League:	315	-
FA Cup:	39	-
Other:	16	-
Total:	370	-

Goalkeeper Joe Reader, who was nicknamed 'Kicker', has the distinction of being the only player to have played for Albion on three different home grounds: Four Acres, Stoney Lane and The Hawthorns.

Ranked one of the finest custodians of his day and an England international, he was awarded one cap, against Ireland in 1894. Reader wore long white trousers until well into the 1890s and it is thought that he was possibly the last footballer to discard them at senior level.

A fine positional 'keeper, he was a superb handler of the ball, had marvellous reflexes and was smart on and off his line – although he often used his feet to good effect when keeping out ground shots. He played in the 1892 and 1895 FA Cup finals for Albion, gaining a winners' medal in the first of these. He also represented the Football League on three occasions and played once for a League Select XI.

In one of his outings for the Football League (*v.* The Irish League), Reader raced out of his goal some fifty yards to prevent an attack developing after the whole of his defence had ventured upfield. He didn't simply whack the ball into touch. He controlled it, beat his man and then sent a forward pass to his colleague, receiving a round of applause for his technique but getting a nasty glance from the bench!

In a League game for Albion he did the same sort of thing, but on this occasion was almost caught out. In April 1895, during the away match at Bolton, he raced twenty yards outside his area to fly-kick the ball away from an opposing player. The ball, however, rebounded off the knee of Bolton's centre forward Billy Joyce and shot towards the unguarded goal. Thankfully Billy Williams, the Albion full-back was quick to sense the danger and saved any embarrassment.

Albion's first-choice 'keeper for sixteen years, having replaced fellow international Bob Roberts, he was forced to give up the game through illness rather than age and some years later he admitted that he would loved to have carried on until he was at least forty.

Reader, who was born in West Bromwich in February 1866, was a dedicated club man who made well over 350 senior appearances for Albion and once played in goal with his arm in a sling! He joined Albion in January 1885 and was associated with the club for a total of sixty-five years, initially as a player until April 1901 (when he was replaced by Ike Webb), then as trainer/coach and finally as a steward until 1950. He held the long service record for half a century until it was surpassed by former secretary and director Alan Everiss.

Reader died in West Bromwich in March 1954.

Football League:	233+4	82
FA Cup:	25	10
League Cup:	27+1	16
Europe:	10	3
Other:	2	1
Total:	297+5	112

One of the great goalscorers of the late 1970s and '80s, Cyrille 'Smokin Joe' Regis made a rapid rise from non-League football with the Isthmian side Hayes to reach the FA Cup semi-final with West Bromwich Albion in the space of eight months – and even by that time he was already marked down as being England's next centre forward.

Born in Maripiasoula, French Guyana in February 1958, Cyrille cost Albion a mere £5,000 in May 1977, after the club's then scouting consultant (and future manager) Ronnie Allen had been informed of his undoubted potential. In fact, Allen, the former England and Baggies centre forward of the 1950s, agreed to pay the required fee out of his own bank account, so impressed was he by the attitude of the nineteen-year-old big striker towards becoming a professional footballer with Albion. Cyrille had already scored 40 league and cup goals for Hayes in two seasons, with 45 in all games.

Cyrille settled in under Allen's wing immediately and what an impact he made! He scored on each of four major debuts for the Baggies in double-quick time – in a Football League Cup-tie v Rotherham United, the First Division game v. Middlesbrough (a real cracker at the Smethwick End of The Hawthorns), a third round FA Cup-tie at home to Blackpool and also in the Tennent-Caledonian Cup tournament in Scotland. Regis also scored on his debut in the Central League v. Sheffield Wednesday – his first goal in Albion colours, driving home a twelve-yard drive after 22 minutes following a precise pass by Ally Brown. For good measure, he also netted a real beauty in his first-ever away League game, at Newcastle, ably assisted and abetted by Laurie Cunningham – who was to become a buddy and remained so until his tragic death in a road accident in Spain.

Initially described in the *Albion News* as being 'a tough, bustling coloured striker' he majestically powered on, and on, and on … eventually claiming a total of 140 goals in 370 outings (including friendlies) for the Albion's first team, including a very useful record of 112 strikes in 302 competitive appearances. He played in three major cup semi-finals (two League Cup and one FA Cup) and also starred in the UEFA Cup quarter-final, scoring in the second leg at The Hawthorns v. Red Star Belgrade.

One of Cyrille Regis' many fine goals – this one coming in a sixth round FA Cup-tie against Nottingham Forest in 1978.

Capped 4 times by England at senior level whilst at The Hawthorns, he also appeared in 3 'B' internationals and lined up for the Under 21s on 6 occasions. Regis formed a terrific striking partnership with both Ally Brown and Tony Brown and, indeed, was assisted by several players up front (John Deehan and Garry Thompson among them), as he strove on at The Hawthorns, admired by the fans and fellow team-mates alike. In his first season with Albion, Regis bagged 10 goals in 34 League outings and added 8 more in 8 FA and League Cup matches.

Thereafter he rained in the goals, topping double figures each season until 1983/84, his best campaign coming in 1981/82 when he notched 25 (17 in the League). There were some quite brilliant efforts, including outstanding strikes against Manchester City at Maine Road and Everton in a League game at The Hawthorns.

Sadly for a lot of people, including the author, Regis left Albion for Coventry City in October 1984 in a £250,000 deal. Less than three years later he helped the Sky Blues win the FA Cup and added another full cap to his collection for good measure. After 282 League and cup outings for Coventry (with 62 goals scored), 'Smokin Joe' moved to Aston Villa in July 1991. He then switched to Wolverhampton Wanderers on a free transfer in August 1993, joining the Wolves mainly as a squad player, and after 19 games (2 goals) he left Molineux for Wycombe Wanderers, also on a 'free' in August 1994. He ended his senior career with a brief spell at Chester City.

In May 1996 Regis became the oldest player ever to star for Wycombe in a senior game (aged 38 years 86 days *v.* Leyton Orient). He finally retired through injury in the summer of 1996, having netted over 200 goals in more than 700 League and Cup games for his six major clubs. In fact, he became the first player to be registered as a professional, and to play at senior level, for these four West Midlands clubs: Albion, Coventry, Villa and Wolves. He also played as a guest star for Happy Valley (Hong Kong) in 1978/79 for good measure.

He returned to his first love, West Bromwich Albion, as reserve team coach in the summer of 1997 under Ray Harford's management, but parted company with the Baggies following the arrival of Gary Megson early in 2000. He was a very popular player, a true gentleman and an incredible goalscorer. Regis is now a football agent and represents, among others, his nephew Jason Roberts, an Albion player in the 2000/01 season.

Bill Richardson

Centre-half, 1926-37

Football League:	319	1
FA Cup:	32	-
Other:	1	-
Total:	352	1

Centre half Bill Richardson – no relation to 'W.G.' but brother to Sammy – was a splendid defender who was unflagging and generally reliable, although perhaps a shade too casual at times. He gave Albion excellent service, appearing in over 350 first-class games and starring in two FA Cup finals (a winner in 1931, a loser in 1935).

Richardson scored only one goal for Albion ... in a local derby against arch rivals Wolves at The Hawthorns in October 1936. It was his 338th appearance for the club at senior level and he found the net in a hard-earned 2-1 victory.

He came close to adding to his tally soon afterwards – in a 7-1 FA Cup win over Spennymoor United – but this time the woodwork prevented his flying header from finding its target.

More crucial, however, were the many times Richardson was on hand at the opposite end of the field to clear danger when his 'keeper was beaten. Twice in a matter of minutes during the home game with Aston Villa in December 1933, he hoofed the ball off his own line in Albion's 2-1 success.

Born in Great Bridge in February 1908, he joined Albion from local junior football in November 1926. After spending two years in the reserves, he finally established himself in the senior side at the expense of Harry Chambers, who had been used as a makeshift pivot following an injury to Joe Evans. Richardson bedded down quickly and, with Tommy Magee on his right and Len Darnell to his left, was part of a formidable midfield line-up. When Evans returned to first team action in March 1929, Richardson moved to right-half, but after a season and a bit he reverted back to the centre position, where he stayed as the Baggies completed the FA Cup and promotion double in 1930/31.

Richardson had an outstanding campaign at the heart of the defence in that incredibly successful season, and some local reporters thought he may well have been considered by England. Over the next six years he continued to defend resolutely before losing his place to Teddy Sandford, who was switched from inside left to the centre half berth. At this point, Richardson moved to Swindon Town. He later returned to the Black Country, where he ended his career with spells at Dudley Town and Vono Sports, retiring in June 1941. He died in West Bromwich in June 1985. Bill and his brother, Sammy, were together at The Hawthorns in the 1926/27 season.

Billy 'W.G.' Richardson

Centre forward, 1929-45

Football League:	320	202
FA Cup:	34	26
Other:	90	100
Total:	444	328

Football League debut in a 6-1 home win over Millwall six months after joining the club. This was the first of more than 300 goals he was to score for the Baggies (202 coming in the Football League, making him the first Albion player to reach a double century).

A headline-maker seemingly every month, he eventually took over from Cookson in Albion's front-line and went on to record many fine scoring achievements. He netted twice in the 1931 FA Cup final win over Birmingham and then sealed promotion with a winning goal in the last League game of that season against Charlton. He claimed four goals in five minutes at West Ham in November 1931, notched three goals in six minutes against Derby County in 1933 and cracked home four more when Albion beat Aston Villa 7-0 away in October 1935. He went on to bag 40 goals that season – a club record. In all he registered 14 League and cup hat-tricks (including 4 four-goal hauls) plus another 12 during the Second World War, when he topped the 100 goal mark. Surprisingly he was only capped once by England, *v.* Holland in 1935 – he certainly deserved more honours, but he did have Dixie Dean and Ted Drake, among others, to contend with!

A goalscorer of the highest calibre, Richardson took the letter 'G' (for ginger) as part of his name to identify him from the other Bill Richardson who was at The Hawthorns at the same time.

In his prime, ginger-haired centre forward 'W.G.' Richardson had few equals and no superiors. He was a top-notch goal-poacher, who had the knack of being in the right place at the right time. He was sharp and cunning, clever and quick, and amazingly adept at nipping in front of his marking defender to glide a centre past the bemused 'keeper. He also packed a very powerful right-foot shot and was no mean header of the ball either.

Richardson was born in County Durham in May 1909. A one-time bus driver, he joined Albion from Hartlepool United in June 1929 – mainly as cover for Jimmy Cookson, Joe Carter and Frank Cresswell. In fact, he did superbly well in the Second XI, netting 50 Central League goals in his first season, and he also scored on his

W.G. Richardson (left) looks on as the Sheffield Wednesday goalkeeper, Brown, comes off his line to gather a high ball during the 1935 FA Cup final at Wembley.

He was not a hard-working player. Indeed, at times he was 'told off' for his lack of commitment by the club's strict trainer Fred Reed, who occasionally punished him by making him to do extra laps round the pitch after a training session! But like Johnny Nicholls, Derek Kevan, Tony Brown and others who followed him, 'W.G.' was an out-and-out goalscorer.

He wasn't a 'fetch and carrier' nor a tackler. He simply loved hitting the back of the net and how well he did that. Goalkeepers all over the country were on the receiving end of 'W.G.'s' marksmanship and one or two defenders wished they hadn't played in the same match.

Occasionally he would thump the ball home, next he would slide it past the 'keeper or simply nudge the ball over the line.   On leaving The Hawthorns in November 1945, he continued to find the net, amassing 55 more goals in only 40 games for Shrewsbury Town before returning 'home' to Albion as assistant trainer/coach in June 1946.

'W.G.' Richardson was still playing the game he loved when he collapsed and died in a charity match in 1959. He was fifty-eight years old.

Sammy Richardson

Right or left-half, 1913-27

Football League:	191	1
FA Cup:	5	-
Other:	6	-
Total:	212	-

A wing-half admired for his workmanlike displays, Sammy Richardson was a physically strong footballer and an honest-to-goodness professional. He was also dominant in the air and an accurate passer of the ball and gave Albion excellent service for a number of years.

Born in West Bromwich in February 1892, he played for several local teams in the Great Bridge area, including Great Bridge Celtic, before joining Albion on a full-time contract in February 1913. Richardson had to wait until January 1915 before making his League debut away at Sheffield United, but in the first season immediately after the First World War he found himself firmly bedded in Albion's middle line, which also included Sid Bowser and Bobby McNeal – what a trio they were: tough, resilient and totally committed to playing football.

Albion won the League Championship in 1919/20, Richardson missing only two games. He was instrumental in setting up many of Albion's attacks, especially those aimed down the right-hand side of the field. He linked up superbly well with his right-winger, Claude Jephcott, and, with the help of full-back Joe Smith, he was able to create chances as well as attempt to prevent the opposing team from getting their attack going.

A fitness fanatic – he often trained on his own for long periods of time – Richardson was lucky to avoid any serious injury.

He was absent from only eight matches during the next two campaigns before he lost his position to Tommy Magee, who had been switched from the right-wing berth. After languishing in the reserves for most of the next two seasons, Richardson regained his first-team place halfway through the 1924/25 League programme when he took over from Bobby McNeal at left-half and he gained a runners-up medal as Albion finished second to Huddersfield Town in the Championship.

He was back in his old position on the right for the next season, but struggled with his form in 1926/27 and was eventually transferred to Newport County in that summer, having made more than 200 first-team appearances for the Baggies; he had scored just one goal in a 3-0 home win over Sheffield United in March 1922.

After Newport, Richardson had a brief spell with Aldershot before retiring in 1931. He died in West Bromwich in September 1959.

Football League:	189	2
FA Cup:	15	-
Other:	1	-
Total:	205	2

After appearing in 173 first team games out of a possible 177 for West Bromwich Albion following his transfer from Middlesbrough in February 1950 for £7,500, right-back Stan Rickaby suffered a dead-leg in a sixth round FA Cup victory over Tottenham Hotspur. Having avoided serious injury up until then (he had only been an absentee through illness and an international call-up) he struggled through the next League game against Chelsea, missed the clash with Blackpool, but was risked by manager Vic Buckingham in the semi-final encounter against Port Vale. Sadly, he broke down again. Later the injury was diagnosed as a torn thigh muscle and it kept him out of the final against Preston North End. Rickaby was bitterly disappointed to miss out on a Wembley trip. He had played superbly well in Albion's defence that season, when the Baggies came so close to becoming the first team this century to win the double – they finished runners-up to Wolves in the First Division and beat Preston 3-2 in the FA Cup final.

Born in the North East of England at Stockton-on-Tees in March 1924, Stan was the top-performing sportsman at his school, taking all the honours in football, cricket and athletics. At the outbreak of the Second World War he was playing for South Bank FC and during an air raid on Stockton, a bomb hit Stan's house. It was badly damaged and his aunt's place nearby was totally destroyed. In 1941 he played his first game for Middlesbrough, where he became reserve full-back to Dick Robinson and George Hardwick. He also played at centre-half during his time at Ayresome Park, but like most footballers at that time he entered the forces, serving in the Army – a 'fighting regiment' he called it. He became a sergeant and was involved in the Normandy breakout and the liberation of Amiens, Arras, Brussels, Antwerp, Eindhoven and Arnhem. Stan also featured in the Battle of the Bulge, fought on the Ardennes, in Reichwald Forest, did a Rhine crossing and various night patrols in Bremen before learning the war was over when just 300 metres from the German lines. He helped to disarm the German army, went down into Hitler's bunker, did house-to-house searches for hidden weapons and found time to marry a German girl from the village of Porz near Cologne (going after and finding her lost family).

When time allowed he played soccer for the Combined Services XI (he starred in an Inter-Allied Cup final in the Berlin Olympic Stadium, when his side beat a Czechoslovakian XI 3-1). He also toured Switzerland, Poland and Czechoslovakia playing football in the 1940s, went to Gottingen University to learn German and, with an eye to the future, he also studied extensively in the field of accountancy. Back at Middlesbrough he signed professional forms in July 1946 and appeared in 10 League games before transferring to The Hawthorns in 1950.

Stan made his debut for Albion two months later against Manchester City and claimed the right-back berth on a regular basis soon after the start of the next season following an injury to Jim Pemberton against Aston Villa. He quickly bedded in and became an international player, capped by England against Northern Ireland at Goodison Park in November 1953, when he helped his country to win 3-1. Stan learnt of his call-up while playing snooker with team-mate Ray Barlow – he was so surprised that he potted a red, which was apparently something of a rare occurrence. He was unlucky not to have won more full caps, but he did have Alf Ramsey and Ron Staniforth to contend with.

Powerfully built and a strong tackler, Stan was usually reliable and safe with his kicking and very rarely hoofed the ball aimlessly downfield unless under severe pressure. A fine positional player, he was only cautioned twice in his entire career, never sent off and the injury he suffered in 1954 not only kept him out of the FA Cup final, but it also prevented him from joining the England World Cup squad. He never let Albion down, going on to make over 200 first-class appearances before losing his place to Welsh international Stuart Williams in March 1955 – this was after a series of poor performances by the team, not by Stan himself.

He was transfer-listed by manager Vic Buckingham at the end of that season. Although still only thirty-one, he chose to quit League football to join Poole Town as player-manager, later assisting Weymouth and Newton Abbot Spurs and becoming a sales director in Devon and later in Cambridge. He joined and subsequently became a director of IOS (Investors Overseas Services) UK Ltd with James Rooseveldt (the eldest son of the US president) before emigrating to Australia and settling in Perth. There he took a job designing kitchens, later managed an old people's home for the church, and helped unite the church with tribal aborigines (he was involved in many hair-raising experiences involving plane journeys, crocodiles and sharks). After this Stan worked for ten years as a probation officer and for the police parole department. He met and spoke with Mother Theresa, had a heart-bypass operation and was knocked down by a car in Spain, receiving multiple injuries but battling on as ever.

Stan is a great character and currently lives in North Beach, Western Australia.

Goalkeeper, 1879-90/1891-92

Football League:	49	-
FA Cup:	35	-
Total:	84	-

Born in West Bromwich in April 1859 and a pupil at Christ Church School, Bob Roberts was a versatile outfield player with the George Salter's Works team before joining West Bromwich Albion as an amateur in 1879. He turned professional in August 1885. After being tried in a number of positions, including those of full-back and centre forward, Roberts eventually settled down as a goalkeeper and was the first Albion player to win a full cap, lining up for England against Scotland in 1887. A fine figure of a man, at 6ft 4in tall and weighing over 13 stone (he wore a size 13 boots), he was daring, agile and very consistent, his reach being his forte – although he did use his long legs on many occasions to keep out ground shots.

Roberts appeared in more than 400 games for Albion at various levels. He won 2 more international caps, starred in 3 international trials and 3 successive FA Cup finals for the Throstles, lining up against Blackburn Rovers in 1886, Aston Villa in 1887 and Preston in 1888, gaining a winners' medal at the third attempt. He had played in Albion's first-ever FA Cup-tie, against Wednesbury Town in November 1883, and also in the club's first Football League game, against Stoke in September 1888.

In the first-ever League season of 1888/89 Roberts was an ever-present, keeping four clean sheets in 22 games. Usually he had Jack Horton and Luther Walker as his full-back partners. They struggled at times and, with Charlie Perry seemingly battling alone at the heart of the defence, Albion had to rely on the courage and agility of Roberts to keep out the goals. If it hadn't been for his quality displays then one feels they would have conceded far more than the 46 that they did give away.

He was brilliant at times, especially when Albion won 2-1 at Derby and 2-1 at home to Blackburn. He did, however, have an off day when Preston won 5-0 at Stoney Lane, making two bad errors, both which led to goals!

Roberts was certainly past his best when he left the club to join Sunderland Albion in May 1890, yet whilst on Wearside he represented the Football Alliance before returning to Albion for a second spell in May 1891, just as Joe Reader was ready to take over between the posts. A year later he switched to neighbouring Aston Villa (as cover for Bill Dunning) but made just four appearances before retiring in June 1893. Roberts died at Byker, Newcastle in October 1929.

Ally Robertson

Defender, 1968-86

Football League:	504+2	8
FA Cup:	34	
League Cup:	53	3
Europe:	12	1
Other:	19	-
Total:	622+4	14

Alistair Robertson had already enjoyed a grand career with the Albion before joining Wolves in September 1986. The tough-tackling defender was born at Philipstoun, Lothian in September 1952, and played for Linlithgow Academy, Uphill Saints and Scotland Schoolboys before spending eighteen years with the Baggies, joining them initially as an apprentice in July 1968.

After winning Youth caps, Robertson made his Albion debut at the age of seventeen against Manchester United. He then overcame a broken leg mishap in 1970 and went on to amass 620 first-team appearances. He was in the Albion teams which lost three major cup semi-finals and was also on the losing side in the 1969 FA Youth Cup final.

Albion's youngest-ever first-team captain when he led the team against Norwich City in November 1972, aged 20 years and 2 months, Robertson was a tough-tackling defender and totally reliable – a player who gave 110 per cent each and every time he took the field, no matter what the circumstances. He drew up a wonderful understanding with John Wile at the heart of the Albion defence. With John Osborne behind him and Wile commanding most the aerial play, Robertson did the business on the ground, relentlessly challenging for every ball, never giving an inch, always committed.

He – and indeed Albion – played their best football under manager Ron Atkinson. Robertson was the tough guy at the back and he loved every minute of it, often battling on through injury to help gain the right result. Hugely dependable, he enjoyed his ventures into Europe and played his part in that wonderful run to the UEFA Cup quarter-finals in 1978/79.

He never won a club medal at The Hawthorns, but after moving to Wolves he gained championship medals in the old Fourth and Third Divisions and also won a Sherpa Van Trophy winners' medal at Wembley.

Robertson was released by Wolves at the end of the 1989/90 season, becoming player-manager of Worcester City and later boss of Cheltenham Town. He quit football in 1992 to become a car salesman.

Bobby Robson
Inside right/right-half, 1956-62

Football League:	239	56
FA Cup:	18	5
Total:	257	61

Bobby Robson started his career as a goalscoring inside forward and finished it as an international wing-half. Born in County Durham in February 1933, he was an amateur with Middlesbrough and a trialist with Southampton before joining Fulham as a professional in May 1950. After six excellent years as an inside right at Craven Cottage (where he played alongside Bedford Jezzard and Johnny Haynes) he moved to West Bromwich Albion in March 1956 for £25,000.

Robson didn't start off too well with the Baggies, being on the end of successive 4-0 defeats in his opening two matches. He soon settled down, however, and formed an excellent striking partnership with Ronnie Allen and, later, with Allen and Derek Kevan, before moving into the half-back line where he became a star performer, driving forward from the centre of the field at every opportunity. During his time at The Hawthorns, Robson won 20 full England caps, playing in the 1958 World Cup finals. He scored over 60 goals in more than 250 first-class appearances for Albion, while serving under three different managers – Vic Buckingham who signed him, Gordon Clark and Archie Macaulay.

He enjoyed his time under Buckingham who, by coincidence, he replaced as manager of Fulham in 1968. In the late 1950s, Albion had one of the finest attacking teams in the country and they scored freely, netting over 250 League and Cup goals in less than 140 matches before Robson was switched into the middle-line.

There he became possibly an even better footballer. He seemed to have a little extra time in which to manoeuvre; he would get forward as often as he could and still managed to score some cracking goals.

His best individual scoring performance for Albion (at League level) was when he notched up four goals in a 5-1 home win over Burnley in December 1957. Whilst on tour in Canada in May 1959, he netted a double hat-trick (six goals) when Alberta All Stars were defeated 15-0 in Calgary.

Albion sold him back to Fulham in August 1962 for £20,000. Three years later Robson ended his playing days with a total of 583 League appearances and 113 goals to his credit. Since 1965 he has been deeply involved in football, taking charge of Vancouver Royals, his old club Fulham and then leading Ipswich Town to FA Cup and UEFA Cup glory in 1978 and 1981 respectively.

He was England boss from 1982 to 1990 and since then he has managed PSV Eindhoven, Sporting Lisbon, FC Porto, Barcelona and PSV (again). He has been at the helm of Newcastle United since September 1999.

99

Bryan Robson OBE

Midfield, 1972-81

Football League:	194+4	39
FA Cup:	10+2	2
League Cup:	17+1	2
Europe:	12	2
Other:	9	1
Total:	242+7	46

After making an impact in the Second Division and then starring in the top flight, and also in Europe, with Albion, the versatile Bryan Robson moved on to greater things with Manchester United and England. He helped the Reds win successive Premiership titles (in 1993 and 1994) and skippered them to three FA Cup final victories – in 1983 (when he scored twice in the replay win over Brighton), 1985 and 1990. He was a League Cup runner-up in 1991, but quickly made up for that disappointment by accepting a prized European medal when he lifted the Cup-Winners' Cup that same season. He also led his country on many occasions, while taking his tally of senior caps to 90 (26 goals scored), marking himself out as one of the finest midfield players in the world in the process. He participated in three World Cups and his international goals included a hat-trick against Turkey in 1984 and a strike after just 26 seconds in the 1982 World Cup game *v.* France in Spain – the tournament's second fastest goal of all time.

Born in Witton Gilbert near Chester-le-Street, County Durham in January 1957, Robson had trials with Burnley, Coventry City and Newcastle United before joining Albion as an apprentice in September 1972, turning professional in August 1974. He made his League debut against York City (away) in April 1975 and the following season helped Albion win promotion from the Second Division under player-manager Johnny Giles.

A versatile footballer, he occupied the left-back, centre half, wing-half and inside forward positions during his time at The Hawthorns. An aggressive competitor, Robson had an endless supply of dynamic stamina. He also had great awareness, and was creative, and possessed excellent passing skills and a powerful shot, not to mention being a superb header of the ball. He teamed up exceedingly well with Giles, Len Cantello and Mick Martin, and then with Cantello, Remi Moses, John Trewick and Gary Owen.

A real body-blow was dealt to all Albion supporters in October 1981 when Robson and Moses were both lured to Old Trafford by their former boss, Ron Atkinson, in a deal worth £2 million, Robson being valued at £1.5 million. Whilst at The Hawthorns, Robson had scored 46 goals in almost 250 first-class appearances for Albion. He had also gained the first 13 of his full international

caps, played twice for the 'B' team and starred in 7 under-21 games for his country – all this coming after earning Youth honours as a teenager. Following his departure, the team gradually fell apart (despite two cup semi-finals), and five years after Robson left, Albion were relegated to the Second Division.

Robson went on to appear in 457 League and cup games for United (scoring 97 goals) before transferring to Middlesbrough as player-manager in May 1994. He guided the Teeside club into the Premiership at the end of his first season in charge and retired as a player in May 1997 with an overall total of 832 competitive appearances under his belt for his various clubs and his country; he had scored 172 goals. He left 'Boro in 2001.

Robson had played for Happy Valley (Hong Kong) with team-mates Tony Godden and Cyrille Regis in 1978/79. His younger brother, Gary, was associated with Albion from 1981 to 1993.

Reg Ryan
Wing-half/inside forward, 1945-55

Football League:	234	28
FA Cup:	20	2
Other:	18	1
Total:	272	31

Born in Dublin in October 1925, 'Paddy' Ryan was a short, stocky, hard-working footballer who played as a wing-half and inside forward during an excellent career which spanned fifteen years. He had unsuccessful trials with Sheffield United and Nottingham Forest before joining Coventry City, transferring to West Bromwich Albion towards the end of the Second World War in April 1945. He gained a place in the Baggies' first team during the second half of the 1945/46 transitional League season and, after making his League debut versus Chesterfield in a home Second Division match on 7 April 1947, he helped the team win promotion in 1948/49. The following season – after a strenuous battle – he at last established himself in the side, making 34 League appearances.

In 1953/54 Ryan was at the hub of the Baggies engine-room as the team went in search of the League and FA Cup double, eventually taking the runners-up spot in the First Division but winning at Wembley to ease the pain. He played in the hole behind the main two strikers (Allen and Nicholls). Ryan often collected the short ball from either Dudley or Barlow and drove forward, either using his winger (Griffin) or supplying a through pass to either of the front men. He and Barlow linked up tremendously well together, and with Dudley adding substance to the midfield, Albion's midfield was one of the best-equipped in the country.

Paddy Ryan – affectionately known as 'rubberneck' because he could leap as high as anyone and get in a powerful header – was not much of a goalscorer himself, but created chances for others. His record of only 31 goals for Albion in more than 270 appearances emphasises that quite clearly – although occasionally he did let fly and netted some beauties! A goal at Old Trafford against Manchester United in April 1953 was one of his best, followed by a fine effort in a 2-1 home win over Blackpool in March 1954.

One of the few players to represent Northern Ireland and the Republic of Ireland, Ryan moved to Derby County in June 1955 for £3,000. He went on to give the Rams excellent service, inspiring them to the Third Division (North) Championship in 1956/57 as skipper before returning to see out his career at Highfield Road. Ryan represented the North in the annual Third Division clash with the South in 1955, scoring from the penalty spot.

In later life he scouted for several clubs, including Aston Villa, Albion, Derby County, Hereford United and Leeds United and also worked in the pools departments at both The Hawthorns and Highfield Road. Ryan died in Sheldon, Birmingham in February 1997.

Football League:	327	-
FA Cup:	36	
Other:	28	-
Total:	391	-

Jimmy Sanders was a marvellously consistent goalkeeper – never flashy and always safe and reliable – who played the last senior game of his career at the age of thirty-eight for Coventry City. Born in Hackney, London in July 1920, and often called 'Cockney Jim', he was something of a penalty-expert, saving over 25 spot-kicks in League and cup football, including 6 crucial ones during West Bromwich Albion's promotion-winning season from the Second Division in 1948/49.

A bomber pilot during the Second World War, he was invalided out of the RAF after being shot down and wounded during air raids over enemy territory. In fact, Sanders was told that his footballing career was over – but he defied doctor's orders and went on to play for another thirteen years! After acting as understudy to the great Sam Bartram at Charlton Athletic, Sanders moved to The Hawthorns in November 1945 and quickly established himself between the posts before losing his position to Norman Heath after a run of more than 100 consecutive appearances.

When Heath was badly injured on the eve of the 1954 FA Cup final, Sanders came back into the side and he went on to help Albion lift the trophy for the fourth time. A famous photograph shows Sanders 'praying' by a post as his team-mate Ronnie Allen scores a penalty to bring the scores level in the Cup Final against Preston North End.

He had a mixed season in 1954/55 but still retained his place in the First XI. He was a regular fixture on the side in 1955/56 and again the following season when Albion reached the FA Cup semi-final, losing in a replay to Aston Villa. With younger 'keepers in the reserves, Sanders proved his worth by producing some fine performances, one of his best displays coming against the Busby babes when he saved a penalty in Albion's thrilling 4-3 victory.

In 1957 the tall figure of Fred Brown had stepped forward to threaten Sanders' position, but the Londoner held on to the number one spot with confidence. It wasn't until the following season that manager Vic Buckingham chose to field a younger man.

After being replaced by Clive Jackman between the posts, Sanders, who still proudly wears his Cup winners' medal on a chain round his neck, left The Hawthorns for Highfield Road, having set a new record for an Albion goalkeeper of 391 appearances. This was to remain intact until Stuart Naylor topped it in 1995. After retiring from football, Sanders ran a number of pubs and also a hotel before settling in Tamworth.

Teddy Sandford

Inside left/centre half, 1930-39

Football League:	286	67
FA Cup:	30	8
Other:	1	-
Total:	317	75

Teddy Sandford had ten excellent seasons at The Hawthorns, over which time he appeared in more than 300 first-class matches and scored 75 goals. He helped Albion complete the FA Cup and promotion double in 1931, reach the 1935 FA Cup final (when he scored against Sheffield Wednesday) and gained one England cap, v. Wales in 1932.

Born within walking distance of the ground in nearby Handsworth in October 1910, Sandford turned professional with Albion in October 1929. He made his senior debut in November of the following year and six months later was celebrating at Wembley with an FA Cup winners' medal. A strong, competitive footballer, with a powerful shot in both feet, he made his mark as an inside left, taking over the role from Joe Carter (who had switched over temporarily from the right flank after Jimmy Edwards had been moved back to wing-half).

In Sandford's first full season, 1931/32, he made 40 League appearances, occupying four different positions by filling in at left-back,

centre half and left-half. In 1934/35 Sandford has his best scoring campaign, netting 20 League goals, the same number as left-winger Wally Boyes and centre forward 'W.G.' Richardson. He was also the team's chief penalty taker (a job previously done by George Shaw) and when he scored from the spot against Wolves at Molineux in October, running repairs had to be carried out to the net before the game could continue. He also scored some goals from long range, one of his best coming against Leeds United at The Hawthorns in February 1936. He netted when Albion beat West Ham 5-1 in London in November 1931 (the game when 'W.G.' Richardson scored four times in five minutes).

Completely out of context, Sandford had the misfortune of being the first Albion player to be sent off twice – in 1932 v. Blackburn and 1934 v. Tottenham.

He was eventually converted into a resolute centre half, captaining Albion from that position when a record crowd of almost 65,000 packed into The Hawthorns for a vital FA Cup-tie with Arsenal in 1937, the year the Baggies went through to the semi-finals.

Sandford left The Hawthorns for Sheffield United in March 1939, but during the Second World War he returned to the Midlands to play for Morris Commercial FC and in 1952 was appointed coach by Albion, later acting as scout for the club between 1961 and 1967. He died in Great Barr, Birmingham in May 1995.

Maurice Setters

Inside right/wing-half, 1955-60

Football League:	120	10
FA Cup:	12	-
Total:	132	10

Bandy-legged, crop-haired Maurice Setters was a tough-tackling wing-half or inside forward, who also filled in at full-back and centre-half during a fine career which spanned twenty years. Born in Honiton, Devon in December 1936, he joined Exeter City in 1952, transferred to Albion for £3,000 in January 1954 and, after more than 130 games for the Baggies, moved to Manchester United for £30,000 in January 1960.

Setters gained England Schoolboy honours and went on to win one youth cap and 16 at Under 23 level, and also played for the FA XI and Young England. He made his Albion debut at Huddersfield in 1955 and gained a regular place in the side in 1957/58 when he occupied the right-half berth, with Joe Kennedy and Ray Barlow across to his left, and had his best season in 1958/59 when he missed only a single League game.

A fiery competitor at times (he was once sent off in an Albion practice match), Setters was certainly a player the fans loved to hate – unless he was in their team!

He certainly relished a challenge, never shirked a tackle and always gave as good as he received – and a bit more as well! He had his ups and down with authority, both at international and club level. Indeed, after a heated row with Albion manager Vic Buckingham whilst touring North America and Canada in 1959, he was sent home. Buckingham left the club soon afterwards, while Setters appeared in 20 more League games before he departed too.

Most Albion supporters were surprised when he left The Hawthorns and one player – his best mate Derek Kevan – was bitterly upset. He almost threatened to quit at the same time but had the common sense to stay where he was while Setters went on to perhaps better things!

Setters helped Manchester United win the FA Cup in 1963 and, after leaving Old Trafford, had spells with Stoke City, Coventry City (1967-70) and Charlton Athletic before becoming Doncaster Rovers' manager between 1971 and 1974.

He then coached at Sheffield Wednesday, was assistant manager at Rotherham United and chief scout with Newcastle United before spending nine years as assistant manager/coach to the Republic of Ireland national team under Jack Charlton.

Setters now lives in Bawtry near Doncaster and does some scouting around the Yorkshire area.

George Shaw
Full-back, 1926-39

Football League:	393	11
FA Cup:	31	-
Other:	1	-
Total:	425	11

Like several of his contemporaries, full-back George 'Cocky' Shaw, also nicknamed 'Teapot', gave West Bromwich Albion Football Club excellent service, appearing in well over 400 competitive games during his eleven-and-a-half years at The Hawthorns. In fact, after making his debut against Sheffield United at Bramall Lane in early December 1926, just after joining the club, he missed only 5 League games out of the next 300 up to January 1934.

Solidly built and good in the air, he kicked with purpose and authority and, besides being able to volley the ball brilliantly, was also adept at taking penalties.

Born in Swinton in October 1899, he played for Doncaster Rovers (two spells) and Gillingham and was an occasional member of the Huddersfield Town team that won three successive First Division titles in the mid-1920s (making 24 appearances). He joined Albion for £4,100 in November 1926, and took over the left-back berth, partnering Bill Ashurst, who was later succeeded by first Bob Finch and then Bert Trentham.

Shaw settled in quickly and was instrumental in helping Albion complete the unique double of winning the FA Cup and promotion from the Second Division in 1930/31 when he was an ever-present, performing splendidly alongside the reliable figure of Trentham. He also played in the 1935 FA Cup final defeat by Sheffield Wednesday. Capped by England against Scotland in 1932, Shaw represented the Football League and went on two FA tours to Belgium, France and Spain in 1929 and Canada, with his team-mate, Tommy Magee, in 1931. Just prior to leaving The Hawthorns he played a handful of senior games with his namesake Cecil in the full-back positions for Albion.

In May 1938, Shaw became player-manager of Stalybridge Celtic, later taking a similar position with Worcester City and then again in Malta with FC Floriana. He was in charge of the Maltese club when they came over to play against Albion in a Festival of Britain challenge match in 1951.

An ex-naval man, Shaw quit football in 1952 and died in March 1973.
NB: Shaw was a dab hand at carpet-making and was also a very talented singer, often breaking into tune whilst on the team coach travelling to an away game. He was joined in harmony by Stan 'the singing winger' Wood and occasionally Teddy Sandford and during one Christmas party the trio went on stage and sang a topical song. When they had finished, they were approached by an agent who wanted them to sign up for a record company.

Football League:	64	46
FA Cup:	4	-
Total:	68	46

Centre forward Fred Shinton was a deadly marksman who would certainly have set all sorts of records had he not left Albion when he did, after just two-and-a-half years with the club. A very sporting character, he played with great determination and commitment, relishing a challenge with his never-say-die attitude. He also loved scoring goals. Born in Wednesbury in March 1883, he played for Hednesford Town prior to joining Albion in April 1905. He was signed by the Baggies as they had struggled to find a steady, reliable centre forward (having used no fewer than six different players in that position in less than a year).

In his first full season with the club he netted 18 goals in 31 League outings and followed this with 28 in just 30 matches in the course of the subsequent campaign – notching up three four-goal hauls (against Clapton Orient, Glossop and Grimsby Town). Initially he formed a terrific three-prong attacking partnership with Chippy Simmons and Adam Haywood and then with Fred Buck and Willie Jordan.

He took the brunt of the challenges up front and always came back for more. When drawn back into defence he was just as tough and determined but he occasionally overdid it with a rather rash tackle. Indeed, he gave away two penalties in one season – both of which were converted.

He loved to barge into goalkeepers and at times took out a defender as well, all three either crashing together on the deck or ending up in the net with the ball elsewhere! His powerful shooting – from any distance – drew gasps of admiration from the supporters and although he missed some real sitters, he also scored some gems, hammering the ball past some of the finest 'keepers in the country. He once burst the ball with a booming effort when scoring for Albion in a 5-1 defeat of Burton United in December 1906.

As hard as nails, Shinton's departure to Leicester Fosse (in part exchange for Harry Wilcox) in December 1907, caused a rumpus at The Hawthorns and it was quite some time before a replacement could be found, Bob Pailor finally arriving on the scene in October 1908. Shinton became Leicester's first goalscoring hero, netting 58 times in 101 games in two spells with the Foxes, either side of a brief sojourn with Bolton Wanderers.

Because of his brave and adventurous style, he was called 'Tickler' and 'Appleyard' at Albion and 'Nutty' at Filbert Street, where he had substantial female support because of his handsome looks. Shinton, who retired with a health problem in 1912, died in West Bromwich in April 1923 after a short illness.

Chippy Simmons

Inside/centre forward, 1898-1904/1905-07

Football League:	178	75
FA Cup:	15	6
Total:	193	81

Born in West Bromwich in September 1878, Charles Simmons was always referred to as 'Chippy' and was a regular scorer from the inside right and centre forward positions for Albion, netting the club's first-ever goal at The Hawthorns in the 1-1 draw with Derby County on 3 September 1900. When he first got into the side, Simmons teamed up with Billy Bassett on the right wing. Then he played in between Tom Perry and Billy Richards in the 1899/1900 season and had Jim Stevenson and Fred Wheldon as his inside colleagues during the 1900/01 campaign, when Albion were relegated to the Second Division.

The following season, Simmons occupied the inside right berth and, with Billy Lee and Tom Worton alongside him, formed part of a tremendously effective goalscoring trio which helped Albion regain their First Division status. Simmons himself weighed in with 23 League goals, including a brilliant hat-trick in a 7-2 home win over Blackpool. A quick, tall player, who was aggressive when he had to be, Simmons could shoot with both feet and was the perfect foil for the much smaller attackers in the side. An England trialist and international reserve on three occasions in 1901/02, he also played for

the Professionals of the South *v.* Amateurs of the South in 1905.

Simmons joined Albion from Worcester Rovers in April 1898 and made his senior debut away to Burnley in November of that year. He remained with the club until July 1904 when, perhaps surprisingly, he was transferred to West Ham United, only to return to The Hawthorns for a second spell in May 1905, where he remained for two more years until he switched his allegiance to Chesterfield Town.

Simmons scored over 80 goals in almost 200 first-class games for Albion – this was an excellent return considering the overall style of play around that time and, indeed, taking into consideration Albion's relatively mediocre form. He used his right foot more than his left, with most of his goals coming from shots inside the penalty zone. He frequently darted forward into space, given the opportunity, and was hard to contain when in full flight. He over-elaborated with his dribbling at times but made up for that with his marksmanship.

His best performance in an Albion shirt may well have been against Barnsley at The Hawthorns on Boxing Day 1905. He had a hand in both of Fred Shinton's goals (slipping the ball through to Billy Law, who crossed for the first, and then knocking a centre back for the second). He scored the other three himself in an exciting 5-3 victory in front of the best crowd of the season, more than 23,000. He rounded off his career in England with Wellington Town before having a brief sojourn in Canada with Royal Rovers, later coaching in that country. He quit football in 1922 and returned to England to become a publican, having first tasted that line of business in 1909. He died in Wednesbury in December 1937.

Football League:	434	-
FA Cup:	30	-
Other:	7	-
Total:	471	-

Joe Smith was a right-back strategist who more than balanced any deficiency in speed with good positional sense. He often cleared his lines with long kicks, aimed down the right-hand touchline. For a relatively small man (5ft 7ins) he was a strong tackler and formed an excellent partnership with Jesse Pennington.

Smith was a very consistent defender, as is clearly illustrated by his exceptionally high tally of appearances accumulated over a period of six years between 1919 and 1925. In that time, Albion fulfilled 252 League fixtures and Smith starred in 247 of them (all in the First Division). He went on to appear in over 470 competitive games for the club – and never scored a goal.

Powerfully built, Smith was never really given a testing time by a left-winger. He always held his own and occasionally frustrated his opponent by closing him right down, moving to within a couple of feet of his backside! He played the game fairly, hardly ever falling foul of the referee, although he was severely lectured in a game at Bolton for arguing with a linesman and almost breaking his flag in half! He was never flustered and a true professional in every sense of the word.

Born in Darby End, Dudley in April 1890, he played his early football with Netherton St Andrew's, Darby End Victoria and Cradley Heath St Luke's before joining Albion as a professional in May 1910. He made his senior debut against Bolton Wanderers (away) five months later, kept his place in the side (at Dick Betteley's expense) and helped Albion win the Second Division title that season, having appeared in 30 League matches. He never looked back after that, although injury forced him to miss the 1912 FA Cup final defeat by Barnsley. After guesting for Everton and Notts County during the First World War, he was capped by England against Wales in a Victory international and later added two full caps to his collection when lining up against Ireland in October 1919 and again in October 1922. In between these representative honours, he was a member of Albion's League Championship-winning side in 1919/20 and also appeared in the Charity Shield game against Tottenham Hotspur at the end of the campaign.

Smith retained his place in the side at right-back until February 1926, when a young Bob Finch was introduced to the defence. When that season came to an end Smith was transferred to Birmingham, later acting as player-manager of Worcester City before retiring from the game in 1933. He died in Wolverhampton in June 1956.

Richard Sneekes

Midfield, 1997-2001

Football League:	208+19	31
FA Cup:	7	2
League Cup:	14+3	2
Other:	2	-
Total:	231+22	35

The third Dutchman to play for Albion, following in the footsteps of Maarten Jol and Romeo Zondervan, midfielder Richard Sneekes made a terrific start to his Baggies career, scoring 10 vital goals in 13 League games at the end of the 1995/96 season as relegation to Division Two was avoided right at the death.

Born in Amsterdam in October 1968, he made his League debut for Ajax as a sixteen-year-old, becoming the youngest player ever to appear in the Dutch First Division (a record subsequently beaten by Clarence Seedorf). He then assisted FC Volendam and Fortuna Sittard (both in Holland) and had a loan spell with the Swiss side Lugano, as well as gaining 3 youth and 22 Under 21 caps for his country before joining Bolton Wanderers for £200,000 in 1994. After helping the Lancashire club reach the Premiership, he was transferred to The Hawthorns for £400,000 in March 1996 and was generally been a marvellous competitor, scoring some cracking goals, most of them from outside the penalty area. An attack-minded midfielder with a pony-tail hairstyle, Sneekes was a real grafter – an eager beaver in the Baggies' engine-room, he always sought to get forward and try his luck with his powerful right-foot shooting. He looked world-class at times, especially when playing alongside the Italian teenager Enzo Maresca in 1999, but his form dipped slightly after Maresca had been transferred to Juventus, and for a time Sneekes found himself out of favour, and was forced to endure an agonising wait on the subs' bench.

However, he bounced back in a confident mood and went on to have a pretty useful 2000/01 campaign, helping Albion reach the First Division play-offs. Unfortunately Bolton Wanderers, Sneekes' old club, prevented the Baggies from claiming Premiership status, winning the two-legged semi-final 5-2 on aggregate (after Albion had held a two-goal lead until late on in the first leg at The Hawthorns). For the flying Dutchman, it was his last farewell, as he was placed on the transfer list shortly afterwards.

During his last season at The Hawthorns, Sneekes passed the personal milestone of 200 League outings for Albion and was well on his way to topping the 250 appearances mark for the club (35 goals scored) before manager Gary Megson decided to release him.

Derek Statham

Left-back, 1975-87

Football League:	298+1	8
FA Cup:	26	2
League Cup:	34	1
Europe:	12	-
Other:	2	-
Total:	372+1	11

One of the finest attacking left-backs in the country during the late 1970s and early 1980s, Derek Statham was desperately unlucky to have Kenny Sansom occupying the same position as himself. Consequently, he had to practically play second fiddle to the Arsenal defender, who went on to win 80 full caps for England against Statham's 3.

With exceptional close ball control, allied to good pace and useful shot, Statham was a vitally important member of Ron Atkinson's attack-minded West Bromwich Albion side between 1978 and 1981 and then again under Ronnie Allen's control.

He linked up splendidly with both his left-sided midfield partner (it was Bryan Robson at first and then Gary Owen) and his left-winger (initially Laurie Cunningham, then Willie Johnston and later Peter Barnes). If there wasn't a wide player in the team then he was quite capable of getting to the bye-line and delivering a positive centre for the likes of Cyrille Regis, Tony Brown and Ally Brown.

Born in Whitmore Reans, Wolverhampton in March 1959 and missed by Wolves as a youngster, Statham joined Albion's apprentice staff in July 1975 and turned professional in April 1976. He scored past Stoke and England 'keeper Peter Shilton on his Albion debut in December of that same year, just a few months

after helping the Baggies' intermediate side win the FA Youth Cup. He played in three losing cup semi-finals for Albion, as well as competing in a UEFA Cup quarter-final encounter against Red Star Belgrade in 1979. Voted Midland Player of the Year in 1978, his first England cap was not gained until five years later, awarded to him by former Albion player Bobby Robson against Wales at Wembley in February 1983. His other two came on tour versus Australia in Sydney and Brisbane four months later.

After a proposed £250,000 transfer to Liverpool had fallen through at the eleventh hour following unfavourable medical reports on his fitness, Statham eventually left The Hawthorns early in the 1987/88 season for Southampton. During his time at The Dell, where he replaced Mark Dennis, he took his career appearance tally past the 450 mark. Statham ended his senior career with Walsall, his 454th and final League outing coming against Doncaster Rovers in May 1993 – sixteen-and-a-half years after his debut.

After leaving the Saddlers, Statham had a brief spell with Telford United and was still playing in local charity matches in 2001.

Derek Statham, one of the finest attacking left-backs in the Football League during the late 1970s and early 1980s.

Football League:	143	-
FA Cup:	21	-
League Cup:	15	1
Europe:	7	-
Other:	6	-
Total:	192+1	1

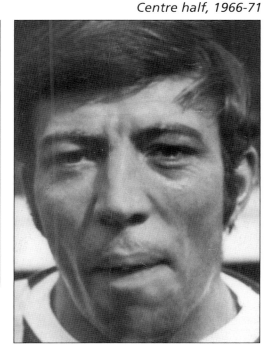

Born in Headington, Oxfordshire in October 1940, centre half John Talbut broke into League football with Burnley in December 1958 after representing Durham Boys. He went on to appear in 160 first-class games for the Clarets and also represented England in 2 schoolboy and 7 Under 23 internationals before joining Albion for £30,000 in December 1966 – being signed by manger Jimmy Hagan as a straight replacement for Stan Jones.

Talbut was a strong, no-nonsense defender, who was both good in the air and reliable on the ground. He repaid every penny of his transfer fee by giving Albion excellent service over the next four-and-a-half years. In that time he amassed more than 190 competitive appearances.

It was very rare for Talbut to go upfield – it was a total surprise to his team-mates and annoyed his manager if he crossed the halfway line – and he scored just one goal for Albion. This was against AS Roma in an Anglo-Italian cup-tie at The Hawthorns in May 1970. Albion won the game 4-0.

After making his Albion debut in the home First Division match against Tottenham Hotspur only days after moving to The Hawthorns, he then had to sit and watch from the stands as the Baggies stormed through to that season's League Cup final, having been cup-tied with his former club. He was obviously disappointed to miss out on a trip to Wembley, but twelve months later he was there in person when, as John Kaye's defensive partner, he helped the Baggies win the FA Cup in 1968. The following season he was a key member of the Albion side that reached the quarter-finals of the European Cup-winners' Cup and in 1970 he returned to Wembley for the League Cup final showdown with Manchester City, but this time finished up with a losers' medal.

Eventually replaced by John Wile at the heart of the Albion defence, Talbut moved the Belgian club KV Mechelen in May 1971 as player-manager. He remained there until 1974 when he retired to become a licensee in Mechelen, naming his premises the 'Kup Winna' (after Albion's success in 1968).

Talbut returned to England in the late 1990s and is now living in retirement in South Shields, the town where he was educated in the mid-1950s.

Bob Taylor
Striker, 1992-2001

Football League:	236+50	106
FA Cup:	6+3	4
League Cup:	18+1	6
Other:	16+5	8
Total:	276+59	124

Following his £300,000 signing from Bristol City in February 1992 by Albion manager Bobby Gould, 'Super' Bob Taylor scored 8 goals in 19 League games in his first half-season with Albion. He then netted 37 in his first full campaign a year later, his tally falling just three short of equalling the club record for most goals in a season, set by 'W.G.' Richardson in 1935/36. When Albion beat Port Vale in the Division Two play-off final at Wembley in May 1993, Taylor seemed certain to open the scoring for the Baggies early in the second half, but was brought down from behind by Peter Swan, who was subsequently sent-off for committing a professional foul. Albion went on to win 3-0.

Taylor quickly became the fans' favourite son at The Hawthorns as the goals rained in thick and fast, from both his feet and his head. Strong and mobile, he scored over 100 goals during his first spell at The Hawthorns – some of them real beauties – before leaving the club in January 1998 to join Premiership side Bolton Wanderers on loan, much to the disapproval of several ardent supporters. He signed permanently for the Trotters six months later on a free transfer, only to return to Albion in March 2000 for £100,000, after Gary Megson had taken over as manager from Brian Little. His welcome return injected some bite and confidence into the side and relegation was averted due, without a doubt, to his presence and 5 vitally important goals. During the 2000/01 season, Taylor acted mainly as reserve to twin strikers Lee Hughes and Jason Roberts, but when called into action he still had a lot to offer and again netted some crucial goals.

Born in Horden in March 1967, he was a trialist with Hartlepool United before joining Leeds United as a professional in March 1988. Taylor scored 13 goals in 54 appearances during his time at Elland Road before transferring to Bristol City for £175,000 in March 1989. At Ashton Gate he added a further 58 goals to his tally (in 126 outings) and was then brought to The Midlands at a time when Albion were struggling to find a ready replacement for Don Goodman in attack. Taylor initially linked up with Paul Williams and then Simon Garner before Andy Hunt arrived from Newcastle United. When Hunt left, it was Lee Hughes who acted as Taylor's aide up front for a time.

During 2000/01 'Super Bob' set a new club record by making the most substitute appearances at senior level in one season.

Bob Taylor – a great striker, one of only twelve players to have netted over 100 first-class goals for the Baggies.

Bert Trentham

Full-back, 1929-37

Football League:	246	-
FA Cup:	25	-
Other:	1	-
Total:	272	-

Never given a roasting by an opposing winger, Bert 'Corker' Trentham was a very competent full-back, able to occupy both flanks but undoubtedly at his best when on the left as partner to George Shaw during the first six seasons of the 1930s.

Born in Chirbury, Salop in April 1908, he played for Hereford United and had an unsuccessful trial with Aston Villa before joining Albion as a professional in April 1929. He made his League debut at Blackpool in March of the following year and established himself in the first team early in the 1930/31 campaign, when he replaced Bob Finch. A model professional and very consistent performer, Trentham was an excellent timer of the ball; he tackled strongly, was sound in defence and tried to use the ball rather than kicking it upfield in hope. He always carried a handkerchief in his withered right hand and very rarely took a throw in.

Trentham and Shaw played together in more than 230 League and cup games for Albion, including appearances in both the 1931 and 1935 FA Cup finals. Trentham missed only 8 Second Division matches in 1930/31 when Albion achieved their unique double. Capped by England at junior level in 1929, Trentham represented the Football League in 1933 and was a candidate for a full international trial but was never called into action.

He didn't find the net in any of his 272 senior games for the club – although it is easy to see why as he rarely ventured over the halfway line.

He did, however, score a couple of goals at top-class level – alas, both went past his own 'keeper, one a misplaced header, the other a poorly angled back pass!

He did come mighty close to breaking his Albion duck (at the right end of the field) with a pile-driver against Blackpool in January 1933, which almost split the crossbar in two, and with another long range effort against Tottenham Hotspur eleven months later which cannoned off an upright.

On leaving The Hawthorns in May 1937, following the arrival of Cecil Shaw from Wolves, he re-joined one of his former clubs, Hereford United, and played his last football with Darlaston before retiring in 1942.

In later life Trentham opened an ironmongery in Ward End, Birmingham and he died in the city in June 1979.

Football League:	190	1
FA Cup:	10	-
Total:	200	1

Jack Vernon was one of the finest players at centre half in European football during the immediate post-war years. In his size 4 boots, he was masterful on the ground, competing with and often dominating the best strikers around. Cool under pressure, Vernon was as steady as a rock at the heart of the Albion defence and a true sportsman of the highest degree.

Born in Belfast in September 1919, he played for Springfield Road Juniors and Dundela Juniors before going to Anfield for a trial. Unsuccessful with Liverpool, he joined Belfast Celtic in 1938, where he became a defender of international quality. He gained three Irish Cup winners' medals (in 1941, 1943 and 1944), two Irish League Championship medals (in 1939 and 1940) and also played for an Irish Select XI on three occasions, as well as representing the Irish League 12 times between 1941 and 1946.

Albion, who had lacked a quality centre half for some years, swooped to sign Vernon for a club record fee of £9,500 in February 1947, the Irishman agreeing a five-year contract with the club. He kept to that commitment, making exactly 200 senior appearances for the Baggies (scoring one goal, against Sheffield Wednesday on Christmas Day in 1948) before returning to his homeland in July 1952 to sign for the Crusaders.

In fact, Vernon, nicknamed 'Twinkletoes', had to wait quite a while before making his Albion debut because of the Arctic weather conditions which gripped England at the time. When he finally pulled on the navy blue and white striped shirt he found himself on the receiving end of a hat-trick, scored by West Ham's Frank Neary, in a 3-2 defeat at Upton Park. Whilst at The Hawthorns, Vernon captained Albion several times. He was a natural leader and outstanding when promotion was gained from the Second Division in 1949; he was even better when he came up against the international centre forwards in the top flight. Nat Lofthouse of Bolton described him as 'a rock at the back', while Blackpool's Stan Mortensen referred to him as 'a piece of Irish granite'.

During his playing career Vernon gained 22 caps at full international level – 20 for Northern Ireland (15 as an Albion player) and 2 for the Republic. He skippered his country on 17 occasions and led the Great Britain side against the Rest of the World in front of 130,000 spectators at Hampden Park in 1947 – which indicates that he was the greatest centre half in the UK at that time.

He retired as a player in June 1954 to concentrate on running his father's butcher's business in Belfast, a job he did until his death in August 1981.

Albion manager Jack Smith (with the ball) gives a pre-season tactical talk to his three Irish international players – Reg Ryan, Jack Vernon and Dave Walsh – while trainers Arthur Fitton (third from the left) and 'W.G.' Richardson (extreme right) look on.

Football League:	165	94
FA Cup:	9	6
Total:	174	100

A consistent marksman wherever he played, Dave Walsh had already netted well over 75 goals in Irish football (including 60 for Linfield in 1945/46) when he joined West Bromwich Albion as a replacement for centre forward 'W.G.' Richardson.

Walsh made a terrific start to his Football League career by scoring in each of his first six outings for the Baggies – a national record. He ended that first post-war season with 28 Second Division goals to his name and never looked back after that, helping Albion win promotion to the First Division in 1949 when he notched up another 23 goals.

As keen as mustard in and around the penalty area, Walsh had speed and thrust and packed a tremendous right-foot shot. Despite being relatively small for a striker at 5ft 9in, he was never afraid to battle it out with the burly defenders who marked him.

He netted some stunning goals, both at home and away, and also at international level. He was aided and abetted by Ike Clarke in 1946/47, when between them they claimed over 50 goals. Clarke, Peter McKennan and Arthur Rowley (who went on to score a record 434 League goals in his career) gave him assistance the following season and in 1948/49 his strike-partner was Jack Haines.

All these players helped set up chances for hot-shot Walsh, who delivered the goods magnificently. A hat-trick against First Division Chelsea in a fifth round FA Cup-tie in 1949 was quite superb and he also netted a brilliant four-timer against Bradford that same year.

Nine months after the arrival at The Hawthorns of Ronnie Allen, Walsh reluctantly left Albion for neighbours Aston Villa, where he took over the centre forward position from Trevor Ford. He continued to torment defenders and goalkeepers alike and scored in seven consecutive games during the 1953/54 season. He then acted as Walsall's main striker in the Third Division (South) until Tony Richards took over as leader of the Saddlers' attack and ended his playing days with Worcester City.

One of the few players to win full caps for both Northern Ireland and the Republic of Ireland, Walsh scored 10 goals in 31 internationals and was a member of the victorious Eire side that inflicted a 2-0 defeat on England at Goodison Park in 1949.

After his playing days had ended he ran a successful sports shop in Droitwich before moving to South Devon where he let out holiday apartments, prior to his retirement in 1994 at the age of seventy.

Ike Webb

Goalkeeper, 1901-05

Football League:	96	-
FA Cup:	5	-
Total:	101	-

A goalkeeper with outstanding reflexes, good handling technique and expert judgement, the mustachioed Ike Webb was spectacular at times – while on the other hand he could be rather 'relaxed', especially when faced with a one-on-one situation.

He could save well-directed shots with ease, often holding onto the ball. He punched with confidence and could hold his own with the rough-and-ready centre forwards of his era, matching them with the same aggression they showed towards him. Quite often he would come out on top, leaving his opponent on the deck. Strong in mind and body and agile enough to leap around on his goal-line, Webb was certainly a fine custodian and was a candidate at one stage for international honours.

Early on in his career, Webb was described as being a 'big, burly 'keeper with outstanding reflexes and quick off his line'. This was certainly a fair description, and one suspects that if he had been with another club (and played regularly in the First Division), he might well have collected a full cap.

Born in Worcester in October 1874, Webb was employed as a salmon fisher near the River Avon before he started playing football seriously with Evesham Town in 1892. He signed for Wellington Town in 1894 and four years later he entered the Football League with Small Heath (July 1898) joining Albion in May 1901 as a direct replacement for the retired Joe Reader. He had an outstanding first season at The Hawthorns, helping Albion win the Second Division title in style, appearing in 33 of the 34 games and conceding only 29 goals (saving two penalties). Webb, who always wore a black cap, remained a first-team regular until losing his place to Fred Cook halfway through the 1904/05 campaign. After making more than 100 senior appearances he eventually left Albion for Sunderland in a £250 deal in December 1904 and later assisted Queens Park Rangers (from March 1907) before retiring in May 1910, when he joined the West Yorkshire regiment as a catering orderly.

Webb amazingly made a comeback with Albion in August 1918, appearing for the first team in a friendly match at the age of forty-three. He later lived and worked in Hockley's jewellery quarter and died in Dudley Road hospital, Winson Green, Birmingham in March 1950, aged seventy-five.

It is interesting to note that some reference books indicate that Webb may well have played in a competitive football match with a fractured skull, possibly whilst with either Sunderland or QPR.

John Wile

Centre half, 1970-83

Football League:	499+1	24
FA Cup:	42	2
League Cup:	42	2
Europe:	12	1
Other:	23	-
Total:	618+1	29

John Wile was a strong, uncompromising defender and a forthright and inspirational captain, who was the backbone of West Bromwich Albion's defence for well over a decade. Born in County Durham in March 1947, he played for Sunderland before joining Peterborough United in 1967. Three years later, in December 1970, Albion manager Alan Ashman paid £32,000 for his services.

Wile, who took over the number five shirt from John Talbut, formed a fine partnership at the back with Ally Robertson. He appeared in more than 600 competitive games for Albion (719 at all levels) with exactly 500 coming in the Football League (out of a total of 525 played during his spell at the club). He missed only one cup-tie and, in 1978/79, appeared in 75 out of 76 first team matches – the most by an Albion player in a single season. He also lined up at centre half more times than any other Baggies' defender (613 plus 1 as a substitute) and overall his appearance tally is the third highest in Albion's history. He was an ever-present in seven seasons – a club record – and helped the Baggies win promotion from the Second Division in 1976.

A fighter to the end, who never shirked a tackle, Wile was always urging his players on and it was perhaps unfortunate that he never played in a major cup final during an excellent career. He came mighty close on three occasions and will always be remembered for his swashbuckling display in the 1978 FA Cup semi-final encounter with Ipswich Town at Highbury. With his head swathed in bandages and blood filling his eyes after an aerial clash with future Albion star Brian Talbut, who had put the Suffolk side ahead in the process, he manfully battled, albeit in vain, to steer the Baggies through to Wembley. When Albion visited China in 1978 he acted as a great ambassador for English football.

Wile rejoined Peterborough in 1983 as player-manager and when he retired in March 1986 he had amassed 831 senior appearances at club level (it was more than 1,000 taking in friendly matches and a spell in the NASL with Vancouver Whitecaps). After a period out of the game when he helped run indoor cricket schools, he returned to The Hawthorns as chief executive in March 1997.

In the mid-1970s Johnny Giles, Albion's player-manager at the time, said of John Wile, 'If you could play football from nine in the morning till nine at night, seven days a week, fifty-two weeks a year, he still wouldn't be satisfied'.

John Wile was a grand ambassador for English football when he skippered Albon on their tour to China and Hong Kong in 1978.

Billy Williams

Full-back, 1894-1901

Football League:	180	8
FA Cup:	23	2
Total:	203	10

Billy Williams was a brilliant full-back whose career was tragically cut short through injury in June 1901 after a cartilage operation had gone drastically wrong; he was only twenty-six years of age. With a stocky build, Williams was a stylish defender, who was cool and confident under pressure and a fine passer of the ball. He loved to get in a shot at least once during the course of a game and often tried his luck from distance. He once scored a stunning goal from long range (some 60 yards) in an FA Cup third round game against Nottingham Forest. He was also very adept from the penalty spot.

Born in West Smethwick in January 1876, Williams played for Old Hill Wanderers immediately before joining Albion as a professional in May 1894, following Magnus Nicholson's departure to Luton Town. He made his senior debut five months later – against Sheffield United in a First Division League game at Bramall Lane – and held on to the number two position for practically the duration of that campaign, taking over the left-back slot late on. He remained in the left-back position for the next four years, before suffering a devastating knee injury early in the 1900/01 season, Albion's first at The Hawthorns. He never recovered full fitness, his place going to Amos Dunn, then Amos Adams and, in 1903, a certain Jesse Pennington.

Williams, cool and efficient in everything he did and tried to do, was never over-played by an opposing winger. He gave his opponent very little room in which to work and consequently was always able to control the situation. Occasionally he was caught off position having gone forward to assist his front men, but this was only occasionally and very rarely was there any danger, with the covering defenders always ready to assist.

In 1898, a fellow professional said of Williams that he was 'very popular among the players'. He had a casual approach to life but was a strict disciplinarian and would often tell colleagues what he thought, while passing on valuable experience at the same time!

Williams possessed an astute tactical brain and would often confer with his team captain, senior colleagues and trainer once a game had commenced and he had worked out how his opponents were attempting to play the game.

Williams made over 200 competitive appearances for Albion. He starred in the 1895 FA Cup final defeat by Aston Villa, won 6 full England caps and also played for the Football League XI and for the Professionals v. Amateurs. He was given a trainer's job at The Hawthorns immediately after hanging up his boots and in 1910 was appointed Albion coach, a position he held until the outbreak of the First World War, when he took over a pub in West Bromwich. He died in the town in January 1929.

Graham Williams
Left-back, 1954-72

Football League:	308+6	10
FA Cup:	25	-
League Cup:	15	1
Europe:	5	-
Other:	1	-
Total:	354+6	11

Born in the village of Hellan, North Wales in April 1938, Graham Williams played for Rhyl Athletic and was an unsuccessful trialist with Burnley in 1953 before joining West Bromwich Albion as an outside left in September 1954. He turned professional in April 1955 and made his Football League debut in that position later that year – when he had Blackpool and England's wing-wizard Stanley Matthews facing him on the same side of the field.

After a couple of seasons in that wide position, Williams was successfully switched to left-back, where initially he had to battle for a first-team place with fellow countryman Stuart Williams. When Stuart left to join Southampton in September 1962, Graham became regular in the senior side and remained so until 1969, when Ray Wilson took over the mantle.

Williams set his colleagues a fine example with his drive and determination. A tenacious tackler, he packed a fine left-foot shot and was always eager to get forward. He was certainly a sterling performer for both the Baggies and also for Wales, winning 26 full caps for his country – the second highest gained by an Albion player, behind his colleague Stuart Williams (whom he played alongside at both club and international level).

Williams remained at The Hawthorns for eighteen years (the last three as player-coach). He skippered Albion to victory in both the 1966 League Cup and 1968 FA Cup finals, scoring in the second leg of the former against West Ham United when he filled the left-half position. He also led his side in the 1967 League Cup final, when Albion lost to underdogs Queens Park Rangers, and played in both the Fairs Cup and European Cup-winners' competitions.

On leaving The Hawthorns in April 1972, Williams subsequently held a number of positions in football, the majority as a senior coach and/or manager, serving in many different countries, including Kuwait, Greece, Nigeria (Leopards FC), Finland (Rovanieman), UAE and Dubai. He managed Cardiff City in 1981/82, scouted for Newport County in 1983/84 and was assistant manager to the senior Welsh side under Bobby Gould in the late 1990s. Williams now lives in Oswestry.

Stuart Williams
Full-back, 1950-62

Football League:	226	6
FA Cup:	20	3
Total:	246	9

The son of a director of Wrexham FC, Stuart Williams was born in the Welsh town in July 1930. He began his playing career as an inside forward with his father's club and, after moving to the Midlands in November 1950 to sign amateur forms for West Bromwich Albion, he worked part-time for an insurance company before taking professional status in the summer of 1951. He found it difficult to gain a first-team place in either the forward or half-back lines and as a result was subsequently converted into a full-back by manager Vic Buckingham, who himself had occupied that same position whilst a player with Tottenham Hotspur.

Williams never looked back and went on to appear in almost 250 competitive games for Albion before transferring to Southampton in September 1962 for £15,000 (after Don Howe and Graham Williams had bedded themselves in as full-back partners at The Hawthorns). Williams gained a club record 33 full caps for Wales whilst an Albion player, later adding another 10 to his tally with Saints. He made his international debut against Austria in 1955. Three years later he starred in the World Cup finals in Sweden when the Welsh were beaten in the quarter-finals by Brazil (Pele scoring the match-winner).

Williams seemed the obvious replacement for the injured Stan Rickaby in Albion's 1954 FA Cup final team that faced Preston North End, but sadly missed out at the last minute when the more experienced Joe Kennedy (normally a centre half) was preferred instead.

Williams eventually switched over to the left-hand side when Len Millard retired and also to allow fellow English international Don Howe to move in to the right-back slot. Yet, with his namesake Graham also challenging strongly for a first team place, Stuart maintained his form and went on to serve Albion for a total of twelve years before moving to The Dell. He later appeared in the 1963 FA Cup semi-final against Manchester United.

On retiring in 1966, Williams returned to The Hawthorns as Albion's first-team trainer and two years later was sponge-man when the Baggies won the FA Cup (having beaten his other former club, Southampton, in the fourth round). He later had a spell as trainer at Villa Park, managed the Iranian side FC Payhaan and was trainer-coach at Scottish club Morton before returning to The Dell, where he acted as assistant manager/coach from 1971/73. His next appointment was scouting for Carlisle United and in 1973/74 he managed the Norwegian side Stavanger before having a third spell with Southampton in 1976/77, again as trainer. After quitting football, Williams worked as a representative for two Hampshire-based tyre companies. He later managed a transport firm, opened a guest house in Southampton and managed the Saints Old Stars XI. He now lives in Southampton.

125

Charlie Wilson

Inside forward/centre forward, 1920-28

Football League:	125	41
FA Cup:	8	4
Total:	133	45

Charlie 'Tug' Wilson has the distinction of being the youngest-ever player to appear in a League game for Albion. He was 16 years and 63 days old when he made his First Division debut at centre forward in place of the injured Bobby Blood against Oldham Athletic (away) in October 1921.

With his film star looks, Wilson was a huge favourite with the supporters, especially the female element, and gave Albion eight years of excellent service.

An opportunist striker with an unquenchable thirst for goals, he scored, on average, a goal every three games for the Baggies. He linked up splendidly with George James, Stan Davies and Joe Carter at The Hawthorns after taking over the inside left position from Fred Morris on a regular basis in March 1924. His best scoring season for Albion was in 1925/26, in which he netted a total of 17 goals in 30 League games when his left-wing partners were Arthur Fitton and Jack Byers.

Able to shoot from any angle and distance, he was always a threat to opposing defenders and, curiously, always seemed to keep his shorts clean in the muddiest of conditions. Nevertheless, he was a hard worker and a player who never shirked a tackle; Wilson was always fighting for the ball and able to withstand the heftiest of challenges.

A battler to the last, Wilson largely had the pleasure of seeing more tough players playing with him (in the same forward line) than against him. He relied on speed more often than not and was adept at spotting an opening.

A Yorkshireman, born in Heeley, Sheffield in July 1905, he had trials with Chesterfield and Sheffield United before joining Albion as an amateur from Hallam FC in December 1920, turning professional almost two years later. After Sammy Short and Harry Chambers had both staked a claim on his position, Wilson left The Hawthorns in February 1928, signing for Sheffield Wednesday for £3,000 (a pretty large fee in those days).

After being converted into a left-half, he moved from Hillsborough to Grimsby Town in March 1932, was a reserve with Aston Villa from August 1933 to April 1934 and rounded off his senior career with a season at Coventry City (until June 1935). He later played at non-League level for Kidderminster Harriers (in two spells) and Worcester City and during the Second World War guested for Aldershot. He then played for Kidderminster Police in 1946/47 before retiring. He later became a licensee in Kidderminster, where he died in April 1985.

Stan Wood

Outside left, 1928-38

Football League:	256	58
FA Cup:	24	8
Other:	1	-
Total:	281	66

Left-winger Stan Wood was nicknamed 'Splinter' (for obvious reasons) and was also known as the 'singing winger' for his renditions of various songs while soaking in the dressing room bath.

A clever ball player, he used to hold his position close to the touchline and often tried to dribble past his opponent rather than beating him for speed, although he was pretty quick over 20 to 25 yards.

He established himself in the first team at The Hawthorns five months after joining Albion from non-League Winsford United, taking over on the left-wing position from Arthur Fitton just three games into the 1928/29 season.

With the exception of the occasional injury and a brief loss of form, he held his place in the side until 1934 (when Wally Boyes took over the mantle), forming an excellent partnership with Teddy Sandford during from 1930 onwards.

Born in Winsford, Cheshire in July 1905, Wood spent two years with his hometown club before moving to The Hawthorns in April 1928 for just £200. For an out-and-out winger, he drew up a very fine scoring record with Albion and besides his own tally of goals, he set up many more for his colleagues with his accurate and intelligent crosses.

A key member of Albion's double-winning side in 1930/31, he missed only one League game, scored 13 goals (some of which were vitally important) and played in all nine FA Cup matches. It was Wood who found space to grab the winning goal in a fourth round home win over Tottenham Hotspur, netting at a crucial stage of the game when Albion were under pressure and finding it hard to breakdown a well-organised defence.

Wood then scored Albion's opening goal at the start of the 1931/32 season, earning them a 1-0 victory at Arsenal in their first game back in the top flight since 1927. He enjoyed playing in the First Division and gave a few international full-backs a testing time with his enterprising wing play.

On leaving Albion in May 1938, he joined Halifax Town and played in every wartime season for the Yorkshire club as well as guesting for Huddersfield Town in 1941/42. He became player-trainer at The Shay from 1946, finally quitting football three years later. Wood died in Halifax in February 1967.

George Woodhall
Outside right/inside right, 1883-92

Football League:	44	10
FA Cup:	30	10
Total:	74	20

Nicknamed 'Spry', George Woodhall was indeed a sprightly player, able to occupy the outside right, inside right and centre forward positions with conviction. A positive player he always had an eye for goal. As a winger he crossed with great accuracy and as an inside or centre forward his shooting was strong and direct.

Born in West Bromwich in September 1863, Woodhall joined Albion in May 1883, turned professional two years later and remained at the club until July 1892, when he was transferred to neighbouring Wolverhampton Wanderers.

He linked up especially well with 'Jem' Bayliss (initially) and then Billy Bassett and with the latter star formed a tremendous right-wing partnership with Albion. They played together in the 1888 FA Cup final victory over Preston North End, when Woodhall scored the decisive second goal, and were then enthusiastic competitors together over the next three seasons before Sammy Nicholls and Roddy McLeod came into the reckoning. Woodhall also played in the losing FA Cup finals of 1886 and 1887 and won 2 England caps in 1888.

He claimed many crucial goals in League and local cup football, had a delightful personality and was a wholehearted sportsman, who retired in 1898 after spells in non-League football with Berwick Rangers (Worcester) and Oldbury Town.

Woodhall was one of the most popular players of the Victorian era. He simply enjoyed playing and when he was sidelined through injury (and that was very rarely) he would still attend matches (both at home and away) and was often seen near the touchline, passing on tips to his team-mates.

If there wasn't a first-team match in progress, he would go and watch the reserves and if they weren't playing, he would select a local match and if he spotted a useful looking footballer, then Albion were always the first to know.

Woodhall almost became a politician, but he withdrew his application when someone told him that he had to work on a Saturday!

George Woodhall died in West Bromwich in September 1924.